World of Manick Sorcar: Where Art Becomes Magic

by

Roma Sur

With foreword by
Patrick Murphy

Galaxylight Books

Library of Congress Cataloging in Publication Data
Roma Sur
World of Manick Sorcar: Where Art Becomes Magic
Library of Congress Control Number: 2008934895
ISBN 978-1-60725-289-4

Copyright © 2009 by publisher. All rights reserved.
No part of this publication may be reproduced, stored
in retrieval system, or transmitted, in any form or by
any means, electronic, mechanical, photocopying,
digital, recording or otherwise, without the prior written
permission of the publisher.

Publisher:

Galaxylight Books
6637 Ingalls Court
Arvada, CO 80003, USA
www.galaxylightbooks.com
Printed in China

Contents

FOREWORD 5

OVERTURE 7

TIMELINE 11

ACT ONE: *Engineer* 16

ROOTS OF ENGINEERING 18

ENGINEERS AT WORK 19

CONCEPTUAL RENDERINGS 20

PROJECTS 21

SORCAR'S SKYLINE 28

BOOKS 30

ACT TWO: *Artist* 34

FOLK ART 37

PAINTING WITH MARKERS 39

NEWS ART 41

TILE ART 50

SLATE ART 53

TILE COLLAGE ART 60

DIGITAL ART 64

ASSORTED ART 71

VARIOUS ART EXHIBITIONS 80

ART IN ARCHITECTURE 81

ACT THREE: *Cartoonist* 88

CARTOONS 90

BOOKS 105

ACT FOUR: *Animator* 106

SORCAR'S MUSIC 108

DEEPA & RUPA: A FAIRY TALE FROM INDIA 112

THE SAGE & THE MOUSE 122

SNIFF (GANDHABICHAR) 126

THE WOODCUTTER'S DAUGHTER 129

RULE OF TWENTY-ONE (EKUSHE AINE) 133

SORCAR ANIMATION PRODUCTS 141

UPCOMING PROJECTS 142

ACT FIVE: *Laserist* 146

LASER ART 148

LASER SHOWS 162

LIVE ACTION SHOWS 178

LASER & LIVE ACTION 185

VOICE OF AMERICA 206

VOICES OF COLORADO & INDIA 207

FINAL ACT: *Family Moments* 208

THEN 208

NOW 209

Foreword

In the world of laser displays, there are many producers and few true artists. Manick Sorcar is definitely in the leading ranks of laser artists. He blends the technical skill necessary to wrangle insubstantial light photons, and the artistic skill to create sublime drawings. In fact, he has not only skill in creating a single drawing or beam pattern, but also the rare ability to sequence these over time to effectively tell a story or evoke an emotion. Through laser, he took his animation skill to another level.

In a curious way, Manick's laser work is perhaps most similar to his work using newspaper clippings, or seeds or even painting on peanuts and rice grains. The media for these are very limited, as is the media for laser. Manick begins with just a dot of light. Two mirrors, each smaller than a penny, move the light from side-to-side and up-and-down. To create flat drawings (laser graphics), the mirrors are aimed at a wall. To create mid-air beam patterns, the mirrors are aimed over the audience.

In both cases, a computer is used to tell the mirrors where and when to move. Literally, the computer "connects the dots" so the beam traces out a vector path. Remember, this is not standard computer graphics (raster or TV-like). This is like an Etch-A-Sketch using light, since laser show graphics are almost always cartoon-like outlines. The artist usually starts with drawing on paper, which is then digitized into the point-path ultimately created by moving mirrors.

Manick's genius is to turn these outlines into compelling images. This can be seen in his "Reflection," which is already a classic. It received first place in the 2007 ILDA Artistic Awards for Laser Photography, and was chosen as the cover art for our 2008 magazine, *The Laserist*. Manick Sorcar's "Reflection" is a combination of beautiful drawing and clever engineering. A single click of the shutter captures a scene that perhaps only Manick could conceive of for its elegant simplicity. His other laser works, such as "Silhouette," also use light in unique ways rarely seen in our industry.

I first met Manick in 2006, when he and his wife, Shikha, came to Rimini, Italy to receive the first place ILDA Artistic Award for best use of laser in a Live Stage Show, for "Enlightenment of Buddha." I was struck by his simple speech and gracious manner. At the time, I thought he was like some ILDA members—a person with a day job who did a few laser things at night. Little did I know the depths of the "day job" and the scope of the "things at night." I realized that, like an onion, Manick is a man of many layers. Each is impressive in its own right. The combination is unique. Frankly, I do not understand how he has the time and energy for all of his projects!

A successful laser show company has experts in technical fields, drawing, digitizing, animation, show production, and even marketing. To find all of these in one person—with such high quality and production values—is amazing. ILDA is fortunate to have Manick Sorcar gracing us with his work. India, America and the world are fortunate to experience the unique media of laser, through the vision of Manick Sorcar.

- Patrick Murphy

Patrick Murphy is the Executive Director of the International Laser Display Association. His special interest is the history and aesthetics of laser art, which he has studied since 1979. He holds a B.A. in Laser Art and Technology from Oberlin College of Ohio, an M.B.A. from Keller Graduate School, and is the recipient of the 2004 ILDA Career Achievement Award.

Overture

I was a student filmmaker at the University of Denver in 2001 when I first met Manick Sorcar. The assignment we had been given was to interview a celebrity and film a two-minute sequence, featuring some of his prominent work. I knew instantly that my ideal subject would be Prafulla Chandra Sorcar, better known by his nickname "Manick." His work was an inspiration to many, and I was seeking an opportunity to meet him.

DU film crew shooting Sorcar in his studio for the project, "The Genius of Manick Sorcar."

Manick Sorcar is a famous animator whose international, award-winning short films were regularly featured on television channels

The entryway into the beautiful Sorcar home.

and religiously watched by children in the community. I was thrilled when he agreed and invited me to conduct the interview in his home. Armed with my JVC camera, lighting gear, notepad, and my crew, I walked up the beautiful driveway, eager to meet the man I had heard so much about. I was immediately awestruck by the elegant Mughal architecture and the sweeping stucco exterior of the Sorcar residence. I couldn't help but stop to notice the gorgeous floral patterns on the steps to his home. The artistic patterns reminded me of my roots in India—it is the Indian way of welcoming guests.

Portico of Sorcar residence.

Ganesha

Sorcar greeted us at the door, with a luminous smile and gentle demeanor. We entered a cool, marble-tiled foyer that was graced by the sculpture of Lord Ganesha, the Hindu God of wisdom and prosperity, carved out of the trunk of a mango tree from India. As I walked through the house—that I later learned he had designed himself—I felt like Alice in "Sorcarland." From the shimmering 20-foot chandelier to large sculptures depicting stories from Indian history, the Sorcar home was a magnificent piece of art, all meticulously reflecting the personality of its creator. The house included many styles of art I had never seen before, such as tiny paintings drawn on grains of rice, and composite photos of celebrities made from newspaper clippings about that individual. It turned out that in his desire to bring Indian culture to the West, Sorcar had created a wide variety of new artistic niches. His studio was packed with international awards for his animated films, laser work, and other forms of art. I was stunned to learn that all of this was done in his "spare time," as his day job was being CEO of Sorcar Engineering Inc., a professional engineering company. These achievements and others had earned him the honor of one of the "Top 100 People" by *Jefferson The Magazine*.

I was overwhelmed and concerned about how I would do

Childhood picture of Manick Sorcar (far left) with father, Late P.C. Sorcar, mother Basanti Sorcar, and siblings: Prodip at far right, Provas in the middle, and Geeta and Ila.

justice to this man's work in a two-minute documentary. I saw in him a man who was never satisfied with his achievements. He was constantly seeking more. Was it art or was it perfection? Or was it perfection through art? How could one man be a full-time lighting engineer, a gifted artist, an award-winning laserist, a world class

animator, and a cartoonist all at the same time? What boggled me was how did he manage to find so much "spare time?" Did he ever sleep? I asked him the same. Sorcar laughed. "That's a familiar question," he said. "If you love what you do, you will find time to do it."

That still didn't answer my question, and I was intrigued. I had heard of great Renaissance men like Leonardo da Vinci, but I had never actually met someone who so brilliantly combined outsize talents for both science and art. As I began my research, I went through hundreds of Internet articles and television specials. Sorcar's life was a constant tussle between art and science. My experience was like being on a treasure hunt, the more I learned, the more inquisitive I became to learn more.

Manick (far right) with parents and eldest sister, Ila.

Sorcar allowed me into his library of scrapbooks. It was a gold mine of information, assembled from what people around the world had sent him. I rummaged through hundreds of newspaper clippings, sepia toned photographs, scrapbooks, journals and family albums. But it was scattered all over like the pieces of a jigsaw puzzle, and I took it upon myself to assemble it into one picture. As I did this, an image began to emerge.

Manick Sorcar hails from the illustrious Sorcar family. His father was the legendary magician Late P.C. Sorcar—the world's leading magician in the 1950's and the 1960's—and Sorcar was the third of five children. As a young boy he traveled the world as his father's stage assistant, which also sparked his early interests in lighting and art. I asked him why he didn't follow in his father's footsteps and become a stage magician. His answer revealed both a great reverence for his father and his own sense of independence. "My father was the greatest magician ever," Sorcar told me, "his legacy is like a huge banyan tree under which my brothers, sisters and I grew up. He trained all of us in the basics of magic. My two younger brothers pursued magic professionally and are doing very well in their respective work. But like my father who discovered and followed his own path, I too wanted to challenge myself to pursue something different, for which I would be recognized on my own merits."

This desire to find his own path is underscored by the fact that he has long gone by his nickname "Manick," which was given to him by his mother. His formal name, like his father and two brothers, is in fact P.C. Sorcar, and his brothers have continued practicing magic under the names P.C. Sorcar, Jr. and P.C. Sorcar, Young. But magic is in Manick Sorcar's blood and it shows in everything that he does—be it sparkling animation, original Indian music, exquisite paintings or amazing laser art. He knows how to cast a spell on his audience, without a wand. Even today, he is silently exploring territories that no artist might have dreamed of, and he has managed to make a mark in each of these fields. Frankly, each chapter in this book can be a book by itself.

The Sorcar family in front of Late P.C. Sorcar's portrait in their home in India.

Over the last 30 years, Sorcar has run his own successful engineering firm during the day but pursued his artistic passions in the evenings and through the night, while most of the world has already retired. "He has a remarkably efficient engine; he goes a long way on very little fuel," smiles his wife Shikha. Sorcar's mind is constantly networking between dozens of projects at a furious pace. Before he can finish one project, in his mind he has already launched into the next one. Shikha marvels at his endless energy: "at parties, in the middle of a conversation, Manick would suddenly jump up and say 'I got it!' If you know him, you'd know that he has perhaps solved a computer problem related to a complex laser effect. Or he would scribble away storyboards of his forthcoming animation on paper napkins while munching on the appetizers." That is Manick Sorcar, a workaholic and a tireless innovator. As a person, Sorcar is a thorough entertainer off the stage as well as on it. He is always in the mood for delivering a side-splitting story and he gets into character every time. He is a man who can find humor in even the most challenging situations. He soaks up every moment of life as though it were his last. His creations are born out of real life situations peppered with loads of imagination, and this is what makes them unique yet universal.

Sorcar with wife, Shikha, and their daughters, Piya and Payal.

Sorcar's work is thought-provoking, diverse, and multi-dimensional, and over the years he has established a series of ground-breaking milestones. For instance, *Deepa & Rupa* was the very first Indian animation in combination with live action. *Sniff* (Gandhabichar), was the very first animation based on a nonsense poem of Sukumar Ray, a great satirical poet of Bengal. *Calcutta Forever: A Laser Fantasy* is recorded as the very first laser documentary ever to be shown inside a professional theater (at the Nandan Theater, Kolkata). *Chhucho Kattaar Biye* (Wedding of the Mole Leader), was the very first and only Indian song to date to feature the normal voice of the singer accompanied by animated singing voices of the animals. He also invented SorcarScope – his unique technique for combining live action with life-size animation on stage. He is the first Asian to receive the ILDA Artistic Award—the Oscar of the laser industry—twice, for his productions *Enlightenment of Buddha* and *Reflection.* But the genius of Manick Sorcar is far from done. Over the years, I have been fortunate in getting to know Sorcar and his works in much greater detail.

Sorcar is an engineer on the outside, but an artist on the inside. He has sought out art in the most unexpected places. Even in engineering, he has been more attracted to lighting design since this is by far more artistic. It turned out that my two-minute interview project was merely the tip of the iceberg. I promised to myself that someday I would try and capture the magic of his work and showcase it in one place. There was no doubt in my mind that the best way to do that would be through a pictorial book since all his work was so visual.

This book is my journey to discover the world of a gifted artist and engineer, as well as a caring family man. It attempts to capture Sorcar's fascinating journey from being a fledgling lighting assistant to a renowned lighting engineer, author, and an award-winning artist in a wide variety of media. It is simply impossible to present all the details, but what you see here captures the best moments from the 1970's to the present day. Sorcar also shares with us the inspiration and memorable moments behind some of his works.

Join me as I step into "Sorcarland"—a glimpse into the remarkable world of Manick Sorcar.

-Roma Sur

Timeline

Prafulla Chandra Sorcar, a.k.a. Manick Sorcar, was born on November 29, 1944 in Mymensing, formerly in India, now in Bangladesh. His father is Pratul Chandra Sorcar, the legendary magician, Late P.C. Sorcar, and mother is Basanti Sorcar. He is the third of five siblings with two older sisters and two younger brothers.

Science:

1960's	Helps in stage lighting for father's world-touring magic shows.
1968	Graduates from Benares Hindu University in Electrical Engineering with First Class.
1969	Electrical Engineer at Hind Motors, West Bengal, India.
1972	Receives a master's degree in Electrical Engineering at the University of Washington in Seattle, Washington, USA.
1972	Electrical engineer at Howard W. Butterweck & Co. in Denver, Colorado, USA.
1974	Company's name changes to Butterweck-Sorcar Engineering, Inc. Manick Sorcar is part owner and vice-president of the company.
1974	Manick weds Shikha in India and returns to the U.S.
1979	His first book, *Rapid Lighting Design & Cost Estimating,* published by world renowned publisher McGraw-Hill Company.
1979	*Rapid Lighting Design & Cost Estimating* becomes a Feature Selection (Book of the Month) by *Architects' Book Club* magazine.
1981	Butterweck-Sorcar Engineering, Inc. commissioned to do the electrical engineering for a grand palace in Riyadh, Saudi Arabia.
1982	*Energy Saving Lighting Systems* published by Van Nostrand Reinhold.
1983	*Energy Saving Lighting Systems* becomes a textbook at the University of Colorado in Boulder and other universities.
1987	*Architectural Lighting for Commercial Interiors* published by John Wiley & Sons.
1988	*Architectural Lighting for Commercial Interiors* becomes a textbook at the University of Colorado in Boulder and Penn State University in University Park, Pennsylvania, USA. Selected as a recommended book by the Department of Energy of the U.S. Government.
1989	Butterweck-Sorcar Engineering, Inc. commissioned to do the electrical engineering for Musashi Kosugi and Shinurayasu—two sports centers in Japan.
1989	Butterweck-Sorcar Engineering, Inc. performs the lighting design for the world's largest concourses, power design for Automated Guide-Way Transit System and airfield lighting vaults and controls—at Denver International Airport, a US $7.2 Billion project.
1998	Lighting design for Colorado Convention Center expansion—a $400 Million project.
2000	The company name of Butterweck-Sorcar Engineering, Inc. is changed to Sorcar Engineering, Inc.
2003	Lighting design for Colorado Convention Center Hyatt Hotel, a $285 Million project.
2005	Honored at Jadavpur University, India, where Sorcar's lighting design books became textbooks for graduate and post-graduate level courses.
2007	Electrical Engineer for Denver Justice Center (Courthouse and Detention Center), a $400 Million project.
2008	Sorcar invited by the Department of Applied Optics and Photonics at the University of Calcutta, India, to be in the advisory committee of the International Conference on Trends in Optics and Photonics (IConTOP), February 4-7, 2009.

Art:

1960's	Helps paint backdrops for his father's magic shows.
1971	*Images of India* art exhibition held at University of Washington, Seattle, USA.
1975	*India* art exhibition held in Chicago, Illinois, USA.
1978	*Folk Arts of India* held at Thomas Jefferson High School, Denver, Colorado, USA.
1983	*The Melting Pot: Indians in America*, his first cartoon book based on the lifestyle of the Indians in America is published.
1985	*Chhucho Kattaar Biye*, a cassette consisting of six children's songs written and composed by Sorcar is released.
1985	*East Meets West*, a half-hour program with his daughters as the lead singers of his songs shown on American Cablevision. The background scenes consisted of his animation.
1986	*Tai-Tai-Tai*, a second cassette consisting of six children's songs written and composed by Sorcar is released.
1986	*East Meets West II*, the sequel to *East Meets West*, shown on American CableVision.
1990	*Deepa & Rupa: A Fairy Tale from India* released on KRMA-TV (PBS) in the U.S.
1991	*Deepa & Rupa: A Fairy Tale from India* nationally telecast in India by Doodarshan, and recorded as the first Indian animation mixed with live animation.
1991	*Deepa & Rupa: A Fairy Tale from India* receives a host of awards including the Gold Plaque (Chicago International Film Festival); Golden Eagle at CINE, Washington, D.C., USA; Nominations for three Heartland Regional Emmy Awards; and Silver and Bronze Medals (International Film Festival of New York), winning over The Children's Workshop's *Sesame Street*, and Hanna-Barbera's *The Greatest Adventure*.
1993	*The Sage & the Mouse*, an animation based on a fable from *The Panchatantra*, receives the Gold Medal at the International Film Festival of New York, USA.
1993	*Sniff*, based on a popular nonsense poem by Sukumar Ray, receives coveted Golden Eagle at CINE, Washington, D.C., USA. It is recorded as the first Bengali animation based on Ray's poetry.
1995	*Spices in the Melting Pot*, the second cartoon book, is released.
1995	*The Woodcutter's Daughter*, based on a story from *The Panchatantra*, selected as a Finalist at the International Film Festival of New York, USA. It was his second animation with live action.
1996	*Images of India: Animation/Transformation* art exhibit held at the prestigious Foothills Art Center in Golden, Colorado, USA.
1996	*The Denver Post* art critics select his art exhibition at the Foothills Art Center as the *Art Show Pick* of the week.
1997-98	Sorcar is selected as one of the "Top 100 People in Artworld" by *Jefferson The Magazine*.
1998	Sorcar's animation films screened at the Denver International Film Festival.
1998	Animation presentation at Place Middle School, Denver, Colorado, USA.
1999	"Manick Sorcar Animation Festival" shown at the North American Bengali Conference in Santa Clara, California, USA.
1999	Sorcar honored by BICHITRA, Detroit, Michigan, USA.
1999-00	Animation screened at Nandan Theater in Kolkata, India.
2000	Animation Workshop: A highlight at the 4th Annual Midwestern Indian-American Student Conference, University of Michigan, USA.
2000	Receives Excellence in Arts Honor Plaque from Congressman Sam Gejdenson at the Biennial Convention of the National Federation of Indian American Associations in East Brunswick, New Jersey, USA.
2000	Art Exhibition at *Celebrate India 2000*, Denver Center for the Performing Arts in Denver, Colorado, USA.
2001	4th Annual Aurora Asian Film Festival features Sorcar's animation.
2001	"Lakeshore Home is Shrine to Indian Culture:" Manick Sorcar's residence gets a two-page cover story in *The Rocky Mountain News*. The house was designed by him, and decorated with his artwork.
2001	Asian Art Association (AAA) of the Denver Art Museum tours the Sorcar residence.

2001	*The Genius of Manick Sorcar*, a graduate level class project at the Mass Communications program, University of Denver, Colorado, USA.
2002	Sorcar's animation highlight the Coors Brewing Co. Annual Function in Golden, Colorado, USA.
2002	Manick Sorcar receives an Honorary Plaque from Dr. Martha Gilliland, the Chancellor of the University of Missouri in Kansas City, Missouri, USA for his distinguished service in promoting Indian culture in the U.S. through animation and art.
2002	*Rule of Twenty-One*, the second animation based on Sukumar Ray's popular nonsense poem released at Uttam Mancha theater, Calcutta, India, and PBS stations in the Rocky Mountain area, in the U.S.
2003	*Rule of Twenty-One* receives the Bronze Plaque at the Columbus International Film Festival.
2005	Manick Sorcar's animation became the subject of research in Bachelor's Degree in Fine Arts program for an American student at the Savannah School of Arts & Design in Savannah, Georgia, USA.
2006	"Laugh Your Art Out:" Sorcartoons featured in *The Statesman*, India.
2006	*Images of India*, Sorcar's art exhibition at the 2006 Arvada Arts Studio Tour.
2007	*Multi-media*, Sorcar's art exhibition at the 2007 Arvada Arts Studio Tour.
2007	Manick Sorcar's animation are aired for the 15th year in a row on PBS stations in the Rocky Mountain region, USA.
2008	Colorado rings in the 2008 New Year with Sorcar animation.
2008	Sorcar's art exhibition at the 2008 Arvada Arts Studio Tour.
2008	Sorcar's art exhibition at Rotary Club's "Odyssey 2008: Share the Journey."

Art Meets Science:

1999-00	Sorcar designs the 5-stage performance arena and directs the one-hour Opening Ceremony of the North American Bengali Conference at the Santa Clara Convention Center, California, USA. There were 70 artists, including Miss Universe Sushmita Sen, who performed under his direction at the hit show.
2000	Sorcar presented his first laser show, *Calcutta Forever: A Laser Fantasy*, at the Nandan theater of the West Bengal Government. The show was recorded as India's first laser-animation inside a theater.
2000	Manick Sorcar introduces SorcarScope, a technique through which he could combine life-size laser-animation with live performances on stage.
2000	Laser-animation, *A Touch of Water*, wins hearts at the Foothills Art Center's Grand Gala in Arvada, Colorado, USA.
2000	*Dancing With My Soul*, a dancing performance mixed with life-size laser-animation performed for the first time at the Biennial Convention of the National Federation of Indian American Association, where Sorcar receives the Excellence in Arts Honor Plaque from Congressman Sam Gejdenson.
2000	*The World of Manick Sorcar*—the mega-show mesmerizes the city of Denver, Colorado, USA.
2000	*Flames of Fusion* performed at the prestigious Auditorium Theater of the Denver Center of Performing Arts in Denver, Colorado, USA.
2001	*Laser-Magic* show at the Indian American Cultural Association in Atlanta, Georgia, USA.
2001	*Rhythm of 2001*—the mega show captivates the city of Denver, Colorado, USA.
2001	*Flames of Fusion* enchants packed audience at the prestigious Auditorium Theater of the Denver Center of Performing Arts in Denver, Colorado, USA.
2002	Performance at the 14th International Congress on Child Abuse & Neglect in Denver, Colorado, USA.
2002	At *Banga Mela*, Manick Sorcar receives an Honorary Plaque from Dr. Martha Gilliland, the Chancellor of the University of Missouri in Kansas City, Missouri, USA for his distinguished service in promoting Indian culture in the U.S. through animation and art.
2002	*Harmony 2002* at Procter & Gamble Hall wins the hearts of audience in Cincinnati, Ohio, USA.

2002-03	*Sorcarama*, an extravaganza of dance-drama-magic in combination with animation, laser and intelligent lighting performed at the Uttam Mancha in Calcutta, India.
2003	Sorcar's show creates waves at *Bangla Utsab* of 2003, Edmonton, Alberta, Canada.
2003	*Synergy* captures the hearts of the Wichitans, in Wichita, Kansas, USA.
2004	Sorcar designs a 3-stage performance arena, and directs the one-hour Opening Ceremony of the North American Bengali Conference at the Baltimore Convention Center in Baltimore, Maryland. It was an extravaganza of 64 live performers in combination with laser-animation and intelligent lighting.
2004	Laser show at the International Center of the Broadmoor Hotel in Colorado Springs, Colorado, USA.
2004	*Dancing With My Soul,* was a Finalist for the Artistic Award at the 2004 International Laser Display Association Conference in Las Vegas, USA.
2004	Laser documentary, *Celebrate Denver,* at the Grand Gala Opening of the Colorado Convention Center in Denver, Colorado, USA.
2005	*Feel Like a Kid Again:* a laser dream at the Pepsi Center Arena in Denver, Colorado, USA.
2005	*Laser Fantasy* at Colorado State University to Raise Tsunami Fund.
2005	*Back to the Future* laser show opens the Gold Rush XVIII Convention in Grand Junction, Colorado, USA.
2005	*Enlightenment of Buddha*, an extravaganza of dance-drama-magic in combination with life-size laser-animation and intelligent lighting performed at the Silver Celebration 25th anniversary of the Asian Pacific Development Center. The venue was the Donald Seawell Ballroom, Denver Center for the Performing Arts.
2005	*Horizon and Beyond*—Sorcar's laser show at I.I.T., Kharagpur, India, where he receives honorary plaque.
2006	*A Painting Brush: Made With Laser*—Sorcar's speech and laser show at Jadavpur University in India.
2006	Sorcar's laser show at the Department of Public Health Engineering in India.
2006	*Enlightenment of Buddha* won First Place at the International Laser Display Association in Rimini, Italy, and was given the ILDA's Artistic Award, acclaimed as the Oscar of the laser industry. Sorcar is the first Asian to receive this award.
2006-07	*LaserToons*, a custom laser show specifically designed for children first time ever in an Indian language, was performed at Nicco Park, the Disneyland of India. A record 78 shows were shown in one month.
2007	Manick Sorcar proposes a Laser Galaxy to West Bengal Government, which will consist of an institution for teaching laser technologies, a theater for stage productions of live performances with laser, and an art gallery of 3-D laser art—all under one roof.
2008	*Reflection* wins First Place at the International Laser Display Association and Sorcar receives the ILDA Artistic Award for the second time.
2008	Manick Sorcar meets Debesh Das, Honorable Minister of IT, West Bengal, India, in Phoenix, Arizona to discuss the possibilities of building Laser Galaxy in Kolkata, India.
2008	ILDA Artistic Award trophy given to Manick Sorcar aboard the *Carnival Imagination* for his laser entry, *Reflection.*
2008	Manick Sorcar's award-winning *Reflection* is featured on *Laserist* magazine's front cover.
2008	Manick Sorcar is featured in Denver's *5280* magazine for his innovative laser art show.

ACT ONE:
Engineer

16

Manick Sorcar's love of engineering dates back to his early life as a stage assistant for his father, P.C. Sorcar's, world-touring magic shows. Sorcar helped with the lighting and art designs of the theatrical performances, but more than the tricks themselves, he was fascinated with the magic that could be created with various applications of light.

His artistic side came naturally to him, but he recognized that science and engineering required formal study to master. He obtained his bachelor's degree in electrical engineering at Benares Hindu University, India in 1968. Following this, he came to the United States and earned a master's degree from the University of Washington in Seattle. He might have returned to India to ply his new skills, but fate intervened.

In early 1972, he came to Denver looking for a job for practical training. He was on an 18-month visa and set to return to Kolkata afterwards. He noticed a job posting in The Denver Post for an electrical engineer with a strong, artistic lighting background. One phone call and a single interview later, Sorcar landed a job at Howard W. Butterweck & Company and his life took a new course.

His prodigious talents were quickly recognized and rewarded. In 1974, after just two years, Sorcar became one of the partners at the firm, making Denver his permanent home with his beloved wife, Shikha, and the company became the Butterweck-Sorcar Engineering Company, Inc. Mr. Butterweck passed away in 2000, and his family sold their shares to Sorcar; thus the firm of Sorcar Engineering, Inc. was born.

Today, Sorcar is the President and Chief Executive Officer of this prestigious firm that has illuminated some of the most famous buildings across Colorado and around the world. Over the last three decades, his work has spanned few hundred thousand to multi-billion dollar projects such as the laboratories for the Colorado Department of Health and Environment, Colorado Convention Center, Denver International Airport, a palace for Prince H.H. Faisal Bin Sultan in Saudi Arabia, and fitness & sport centers in Japan—to name a few.

It is no surprise that Sorcar's lighting designs are a magical blend of engineering and art. His work features cutting-edge technology combined with art and energy-saving techniques which make them functional, efficient and beautiful.

SORCAR
ENGINEERING, INC.

Roots of Engineering

The roots of Sorcar's interests in engineering and art go back to his childhood when he would help his father in his stage shows, painting backdrops and doing lighting effects. It was the "Sputnik Illusion" incident that kindled the fire in him. The "Sputnik Illusion" was an item in P.C. Sorcar's two and a half-hour magic show. Just a few days before the show, the lighting dial, which projected the moving galaxy lighting effect, broke into pieces. The illusion was in jeopardy! Sorcar, then a teenager, painted the galaxy on a mica sheet and quietly replaced the broken dial on the day of the show. It was a big surprise to his father who exclaimed, "now that was *real* magic!" This incident sparked Sorcar's interest in theatrical art and lighting.

(*top*) Sputnik Illusion.
(*bottom*) Sorcar with his father, Late P.C. Sorcar, at Rockefeller Center, New York, USA in 1964.

Engineers at Work

Sorcar started his career in the U.S. in 1972 with Howard W. Butterweck & Company of Denver, Colorado, USA, an electrical consulting firm that was established in 1958. Sorcar's rare qualities in mixing art and engineering were promptly recognized by Mr. Butterweck. In 1974, the company reincorporated, taking him as one of the principals and changing the company name to Butterweck-Sorcar Engineering, Inc.

(top) Manick Sorcar & Howard W. Butterweck in Sorcar's office in 1983.
(bottom) The original building where Butterweck-Sorcar Engineering, Inc. had their company. The building's electrical systems were designed by the company.

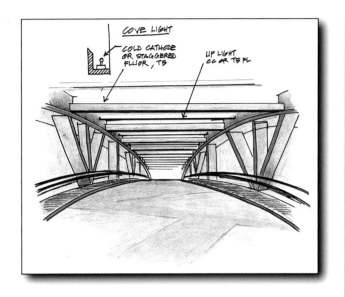

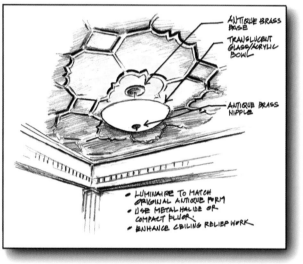

Conceptual Renderings

Before designing any lighting system, Sorcar renders his thoughts on paper. "Lighting design is a balanced mix of science and art. The scientific part is mathematics, which can be calculated. The artistic part reflects aesthetics and the mood issues—it must be carefully rendered in my mind first before I put it down on paper," says Sorcar.

(top) Conceptual rendering and final installation of bridge at Concourse A at Denver International Airport. *(bottom)* Conceptual rendering (right) to actual installation (left). This particular project for East High School's 100 year-old library had the special challenge of designing a lighting system that not only matched the aesthetics of the original fixture, but also complemented the architecture of the era, and produced energy-efficient lighting.

Clinton Terminal at Arapahoe County Airport

This was Sorcar's first airport project in the early-70's, where the company performed the complete electrical engineering for the Clinton Terminal at the Arapahoe County Airport. This was only the first of several airport jobs that Sorcar would work on in his tenured career.

(top) A view from inside the Clinton Aviation Terminal at Arapahoe County Airport. (Architect: Richard J. Frank)
(bottom) A view from outside of the terminal.

Denver International Airport Concourses

In 1989, Butterweck-Sorcar Engineering, Inc. was commissioned to do the lighting design for the world's largest concourses in Denver, Colorado, USA. The company had fused energy-efficient lighting with intelligent light design to illuminate Denver International Airport's concourses. In the interiors, the design was carefully woven so that electrical lighting was all controlled by an intelligent low-voltage switching system, one that automatically sheds electrical light to interact with daylight. On the outside, they implemented a glare-free apron lighting to facilitate safe docking at the gates for the pilots and ground crew. The concourses' total length is greater than the length of five Empire State Buildings in tandem. The $7.2 billion project was completed in 1993.

(top left) Image of Denver International Airport. (Architect: Fentress /Bradburn Architects, Ltd.)
(top right) Manick and Shikha Sorcar, with then Denver Mayor Wellington Webb and his wife, Wilma Webb, at the Grand Opening of Denver International Airport.
(others) Various images of the illuminated concourses inside Denver International Airport. The architects were Allred Fischer Seracuse Lawler & Partners/TRA-Joint Venture, and Wong Strauch.

Automated Guideway Transit System

Butterweck-Sorcar Engineering, Inc. was a sub-consultant to Lea+ Elliott, Inc. in designing the Automated Guideway Transit System's (AGTS) electrical power distribution system—the nerve center for transporting 12,000 passengers from the terminal to the concourses. The AGTS was designed to have a system which included multiple redundancy for all of its components. Today, it transports 6,000 passengers per hour during peak hours. The train and control rooms are on uninterruptable power supply, giving back-up power in emergency situations.

(top) Image from inside one of the AGTS trains.
(left) Late Bill Smith, Manager of Public Works for the City & County of Denver, with Sorcar.
(right) View of the AGTS from inside the tunnel.

Airport Lighting Vaults & Controls

Butterweck-Sorcar Engineering, Inc. was the primary consultant for designing the most sophisticated airfield lighting system ever installed and operated by simply touching a computer screen. With sub-consultants CH2MHill and Merrick & Company, their design included energizing over 18,000 running lights with constant current regulators in two lighting vaults operating from the world's tallest control tower.

(top) A view from inside Denver International Airport's control tower.
(bottom left) Interior view of the airfield lighting vaults.
(bottom right) Exterior view of DIA's control tower.

Colorado Convention Center Expansion

   In 2000, the company's name was changed to Sorcar Engineering, Inc. after the demise of Mr. Butterweck. When the Colorado Convention Center expanded the building to double its original size, Sorcar Engineering, Inc. was commissioned to be the lighting engineer of record for the $400 Million project. This included the lighting design of the new 50,000 square-foot Great Ballroom, 5000-seat Lecture Hall, and 584,000 square-foot Exhibition Space.

   The building's key design gestures along its two main facades: the thoroughfare, along the west edge of downtown Denver, and the opposite side that opens into the heart of downtown. A high-peaked, 662-foot long roof line and full-facade glass curtain wall along the thoroughfare transforms the Denver skyline similar to the Sydney Opera House in Australia. This canted, upward-cutting shape against Denver's skyline is lit up at night, a striking gesture of identity both for the building and the city. The lighting for the massive project was co-designed by Sorcar Engineering, Inc. and LAM Partners, Inc.

(top) A view of the Colorado Convention Center. (Architect: Fentress/Bradburn Architects, Ltd)
(bottom left) The Colorado Convention Center Ballroom consists of over 10,000 crystals illuminated with fiber optics, all programmed to change in color for various, thematic atmospheres. (Photograph taken by Steve Crecelius for Denver Metro Convention & Visitors Bureau.)
(bottom right) Sorcar with Denver Mayor John Hickenlooper & architect James H. Bradburn of Fentress/Bradburn Architects, Ltd at the construction site.

Denver Convention Center Hyatt Hotel

Sorcar Engineering, Inc. was selected to be the lighting engineer of record for the $285 Million project. The 1.25 million square-foot, 37-floor project includes 60,000 square-feet of meeting space, two ballrooms, a four-story atrium, a large health club facility, a restaurant and a rooftop lounge. The lighting was co-designed by Sorcar Engineering, Inc. and ILD, Inc.

(left) Sorcar puts his signature during the Topping-Out Ceremony, where all of the design team signs the last beam before it is hoisted up into place.
(right) A view of the Denver Convention Center Hyatt Hotel. (Architects: Klipp Colussy Jenks and DuBois Architects/Brennan Beer Gorman Architects)

Denver Justice Center - Courthouse & Detention Center

At the time of writing this book, Sorcar Engineering, Inc. was commissioned to do the complete electrical engineering for the Denver Justice Center, containing the Courthouse and Detention Center adjoined by a tunnel, in the heart of the City of Denver. The total construction cost is approximately $400 million and the completion date is late 2009.

(top) An architectural rendering of the Justice Center - Courthouse. (Architects: Klipp Architecture, Ricci Greene Associates and Harold Massop Associate Architects)
(bottom) An architectural rendering of the Detention Center. (Architects: Hartman-Cox Architects, Ricci Greene Associates and OZ Architects of Denver, Inc.)

UNION SQUARE, USA

SHINURAYASU, JAPAN

PARAGON, USA

UNION SQUARE, USA

Residential Building

Commercial Building

CCCX, USA

PARKPLACE RESIDENCE, USA

THE WINDSOR, USA

TWIN TOWERS, USA

MUSASHI KOSUGI, JAPAN

Sorcar's Skyline

Sorcar's designs have reached far and wide, countries such as Mexico and Canada, together with Japan, India and Saudi Arabia. But a significant amount of his work in the U.S. is in Colorado, where he has lived since the early-70's. Under his personal supervision and design, much of the Denver skyline has been engineered and illuminated by his company. Projects consisted of planning for cities, a variety of structures ranging from educational complexes at universities to high-rise buildings, airports, hospitals, bridges and mass transit terminals—to name a few. Each project was approached with cost-effective planning, energy-effective and aesthetically pleasing solutions.

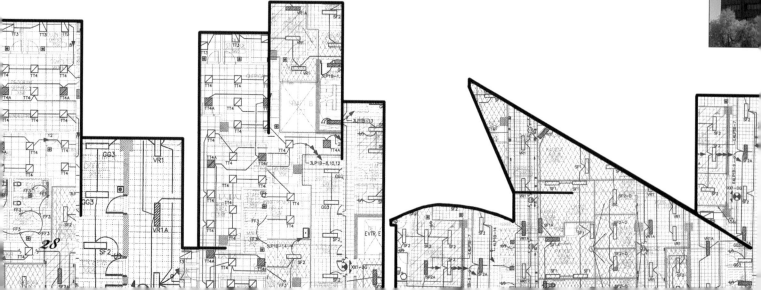

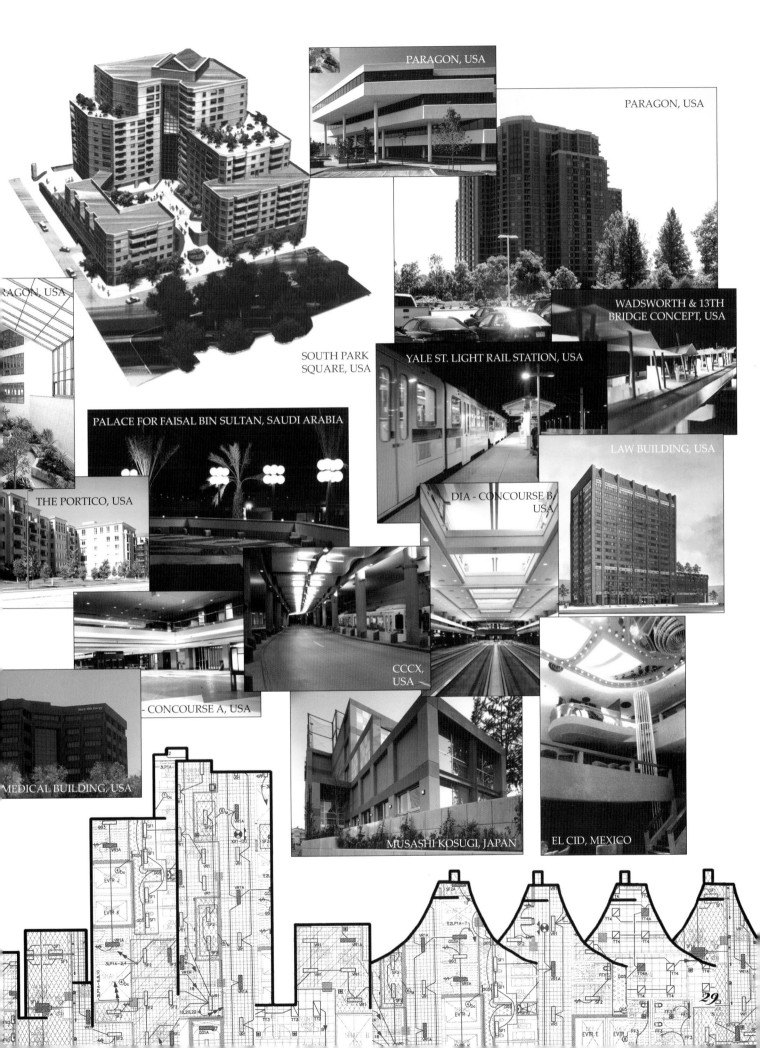

PARAGON, USA

PARAGON, USA

RAGON, USA

WADSWORTH & 13TH
BRIDGE CONCEPT, USA

SOUTH PARK
SQUARE, USA

YALE ST. LIGHT RAIL STATION, USA

PALACE FOR FAISAL BIN SULTAN, SAUDI ARABIA

LAW BUILDING, USA

THE PORTICO, USA

DIA - CONCOURSE B,
USA

CCCX,
USA

- CONCOURSE A, USA

MEDICAL BUILDING, USA

MUSASHI KOSUGI, JAPAN

EL CID, MEXICO

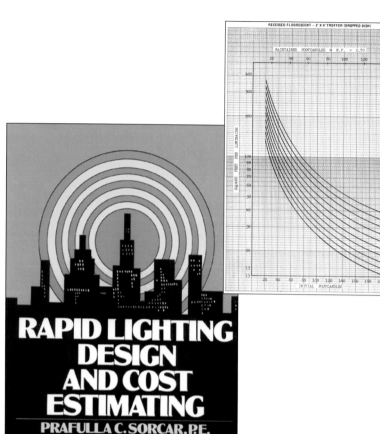

"Here is a handy, quick method for lighting design and calculations of installation prices for both indoor and outdoor lighting projects. With this book, one can quickly select a fixture according to aesthetics, lumen output, visual comfort, energy efficiency, and installation cost without going through a number of catalogs..."

Lighting Design & Application
USA
February, 1980

Rapid Lighting Design & Cost Estimating

Sorcar's expertise in lighting techniques was shared with the world through a series of books that he had written. *Rapid Lighting Design & Cost Estimating* was his first book, and the roots of the book go back to his own notebook during the early days with Howard Butterweck & Co., where he developed quick methods of calculating lighting and cost estimating through a series of curves. The notebook, which was instantly popular within the company, soon went beyond boundaries when it was published as a hardcover book by world renowned McGraw-Hill Company, in 1979. It was a Feature Selection as the book of the month for the December Bulletin of the *Architects' Book Club*, New Jersey, USA. All of the technical books were written under his formal name, Prafulla C. Sorcar.

(top) Front cover of *Rapid Lighting Design and Cost Estimating*.
(inset) Page insert showing curves used for quick answers.
(right) Front cover of the *Architects' Book Club*, December, 1979, with Sorcar's book as the Feature Selection.

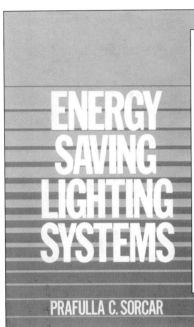

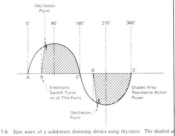

Fig. 7-8. Sine wave of a solid-state dimming device using thyristor. The shaded a...
sents power at a dimmed condition.

drawing the working power. The net power requirement for the dimm...
poses, representing the total shaded area, is much less than would be ...
for an undimmed situation.

The slope shown at the rising point of current at points B and B' re...
the short time interval required to start from 0 to the first peak value in a...
In reality, the current tends to overshoot the curve and somewhat ...
before reaching a steady state. The phenomenon repeats twice each cyc...
results in a radio frequency (RF) noise and lamp filament ringing. Man...
facturers provide RF suppression and have chokes available that will n...
filament ringing.

The new solid-state dimmers designed for incandescents are available f...
to 2000 watts, wall-box mounted type. Although incandescent filamen...
are the most inefficient of all the types of light source, a significant am...
power can be saved by light-level reduction. Figure 7-9 shows the effect

"... The basic concepts that are either introduced or assumed, are always demonstrated with practical examples. Carefully detailed, step-by-step descriptions of the process for accomplishing the engineering design of a commercial lighting system are found... Energy conservation and lighting controls are covered from an equipment-oriented point of view.

The style is clear, the presentation is good, and the references sufficient to help the reader pursue a particular topic. It is easy to recommend this book."

Lighting Design & Application
USA
February, 1984

"... The book certainly deserves a place on the designer's book shelf, among the other handbooks published in this field."

International Lighting Review
Amsterdam, Holland
February, 1982

"I have reviewed it carefully and have decided to use it as the textbook for the second semester of the two semester sequence in Illuminating Engineering that I teach here at the University of Colorado."

Professor David DiLaura, FIES
University of Colorado
Boulder, Colorado, USA

Energy Saving Lighting Systems

Sorcar's second book was published by Van Vostrand Reinhold in 1982. It was during the era of President Jimmy Carter, when energy conservation was the cry of the day. The book was selected as a text at the University of Colorado in Boulder, USA. In the following years it became a text at several universities including Penn State University in University Park, Pennsylvania, USA, and Jadavpur University in Kolkata, India.

(top) Cover and inset from Sorcar's second book, *Energy Saving Lighting Systems.*

"Sorcar has bridged the gap in lighting texts by effectively integrating science and art. Sorcar's educational background in electrical engineering provides the necessary expertise in the scientific aspects of lighting while his professional experience has given him a sensitivity and understanding of the need to access and address the art aspects of lighting... Depth and breadth of material covered in an understandable format are successfully presented. Sorcar has balanced science and art, the quantitative and the qualitative in this text."

Journal of Interior Design Education and Research
USA
Volume 14, No. 2, Fall 1998

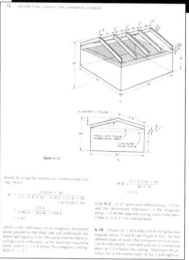

Architectural Lighting for Commercial Interiors

Sorcar's third book was published by John Wiley & Sons in 1987, simultaneously in the USA and in Canada. In addition to the quantity, this popular book took the visual, aesthetical, psychological and physiological effects in the designs for commercial interior lighting. Reviewed by Steve Stannard, Chairman of the Calculation Procedures Committee of the Illuminating Engineering Society of North America and several key architects, this book was also selected as a text for illuminating engineering and architectural engineering courses at a number of universities in addition to becoming a recommended book by the U.S. Department of Energy (DOE) for their Federal Energy Management Program (FEMP) and Energy Efficiency for Commercial Buildings (EREC) Program. It was also a "Recommended Book in Professional Engineering/Architecture" by the Massachusetts Institute Technology (MIT), USA.

(top) Front cover of Sorcar's third book, *Architectural Lighting for Commercial Interiors.*
(bottom) A page from the book.

32

"The son of a magician, Prafulla Sorcar has succeeded in combining useful information about the engineering aspects of lighting with an inspired appreciation for the art and magic of designing visual environments. The book is well-written and clearly illustrated. Text and graphics combine to clarify even the most difficult technical information. Most of the illustrations are hand-drawn by the author, who is a master of the explanatory diagram.. Sorcar has succeeded in what he set out to do, to blend the scientific and artistic aspects of lighting into a coherent and a practical guide for designers. Whether you are a novice that is needing a clear explanation of how to calculate lighting levels or a seasoned designer in search of a combination reference-inspiration, *Architectural Lighting for Commercial Interiors* is an invaluable addition to your library."

Barbara-Jo Novitski
Architectural Lighting
Book Reviews section
USA
May, 1989

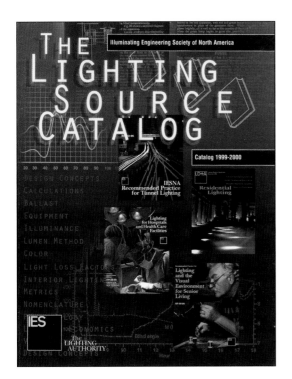

(top) Review of Sorcar's third book in the popular *Architectural Lighting* magazine.
(bottom left) All three of Sorcar's books were recommended by *The Lighting Source Catalog* of the Illuminating Engineering Society of North America.
(bottom right) *Architectural Lighting for Commercial Interiors* was a featured selection on the cover page of publisher Wiley & Son's *Architecture Catalog*.

ACT TWO:
Artist

Now meet the other Manick Sorcar—the one that toils away evenings, nights and weekends. His daytime work is guided by the rules of engineering code and the needs of his clients. At night, he slips into his studio where no rules apply, except his own. He follows his artistic instincts and sets his imagination free in a world where there are no boundaries.

Is Sorcar an engineer or an artist? This is a natural question that baffles many. In my careful study, I would describe him as a man with the mind of an engineer, and the soul of an artist. Everything he does has an artistic touch—whether it is a complicated lighting design or a high-end laser creation—but it also involves extensive planning, preparation, and logic.

On a typical Sunday morning, Sorcar is in his paint-splattered white pants, chipping away on a tile slate or messing around with chicken wire, trying to create a piece of art. I am mesmerized by his heady zest and boundless energy to create art out of nothing. Give him a peanut and he turns it into a portrait of President Jimmy Carter. While we see a pot of Indian spices and lentils as food, he sees an image of the Hindu Lord Ganesha. He has an uncanny knack for picking up everyday objects and transforming them into something extraordinary. In fact, nothing is ordinary to him. He sees the world as a giant, artistic palette with endless opportunities to create. To me, this is real magic. I call it the Midas Touch (it is definitely no coincidence that "Manick" means gold in Bengali.)

Again, Sorcar credits his time traveling with his father and working on his magic shows for fostering his interest in this area. In those days he would assist with lighting, artwork, painting and elaborate backdrops. These experiences triggered his interest in lighting design and art at the same time. Even when he came to the United States, he pursued his interest in art through various art exhibitions, alongside his engineering career.

Sorcar's house is perhaps his magnum opus, with an astonishing array of artwork everywhere. Clay, Styrofoam, tile, Indian spices, bricks, newspaper clippings—each of these has been transformed into an exquisite creation, rooted in Indian culture, but with a universal appeal.

P. C. Sorcar, Magician

Water paint on cardboard (30" H x 18" W)

    Sorcar painted this portrait of his father when he was only 21. "It was water paint on cardboard, capturing the cubical image of him," said Sorcar, "he liked it so much, he gazed at it for days." The picture was published in many international journals and trade magazines of magic, including the publications of the *All India Magic Circle*.

Shringar

Clay on wood (32" H x 12" W)

Thorn

Clay on wood (32" H x 12" W)

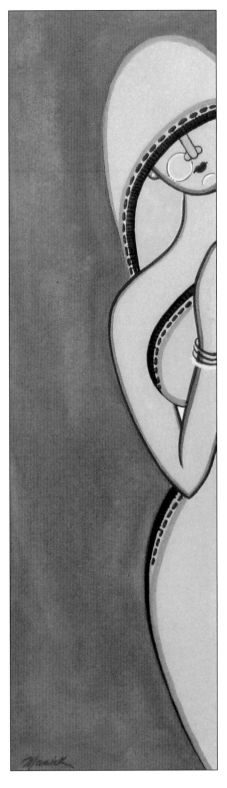

Folk Art

Sorcar's early work of the 70's in the United States was very traditional, consisting of either water paint or acrylic on paper, focusing on rural India for his subject matter. He was particularly fond of painting scenes from Bengal, his place of origin. In all of his exhibitions, he portrayed his love for painting in bold colors through stylized figurines. During his *Folk Art of India* exhibition in 1978, the *Daily Transcript* of Golden, Colorado, USA, wrote, "the folk paintings of Manick Sorcar in bold acrylics, are a kind of latter-day tributary to the mainstream of Indian folk art, an ancient and continuous flow."

His other works included clay sculptures on wood, and incorporated a wide range of media into the pieces, such as fabric, stray paper, along with acrylic paints.

Shy

Acrylic on paper (26" H x 11" W)

Bangalalana (A Bengali Lady)

Mixed media—acrylic, fabric, and grass cloth. (21″ H x 20″ W)

Mr. Banyan

Marker on newsprint (17.5″ H x 22″ W)

Rupa's Home

Marker on newsprint (17.5″ H x 22″ W)

Painting With Markers

In the mid-80's, Sorcar introduced yet another type of artwork which he used extensively for the background scenes of his hit animation, *Deepa & Rupa: A Fairy Tale From India*. What made these so special is that each of them was painted with oil-based markers on newsprint—a technique that he developed to avoid wrinkles on the paper—a traditional problem that occurred with water paints. The scenes were then "frame-grabbed" by a digital camera to be combined with his animation. For its artwork, the film was nominated for a Heartland Regional Emmy award in 1990.

Rural Home

Marker on newsprint (17.5″ H x 22″ W)

Enchanting Path

Marker on newsprint (17.5″ H x 22″ W)

Bridge over Drain

Marker on newsprint (17.5″ H x 22″ W)

"Despite what a few highfalutin' journalists might say, there aren't many of us who would confuse newspaper clippings with art, unless those clippings end up in the hands of artist, animator, and lighting designer, Manick Sorcar. .. Then they become portraits of Mahatma Gandhi, John F. Kennedy, or even former Denver mayor, Wellington Webb."

The Denver Post
USA
October 23, 1996

The portrait of Mahatma Gandhi was created with newspaper clippings of sixteen popular languages in India: Punjabi, Sindhi, Gujarati, Marathi, Kashmiri, Oriya, Bengali, Kannarees, Tamil, Malayalam, Telugu, Assamese, Urdu, Sanskrit, Hindi, and English. Name of the piece: "Our Gandhi."

Our Gandhi

Newsclip Collage (21" H x 17" W)

News Art

In the 90's, Sorcar introduced another type of artwork: News Art, which was originated by him and to the best of my knowledge, he is the only one who still does this kind of art. His raw material was a collection of newspaper clippings which he collaged to become the subject in the newspaper. "At first I used random newspaper articles to create the portraits, but I had really wanted to make each one an authentic piece of world history. So, I started collecting articles about the subjects for months, having enough to finally collage the image to create a piece of history, " says Sorcar.

A little bit of magic with Manick-touch! His father used to tear apart a newspaper and then restore it by magic. Manick Sorcar's abracadabra goes a step further—it becomes a portrait!

President John F. Kennedy

Newsclip Collage (21" H x 20" W)

The portraits of President John F. Kennedy and First Lady Jackie Kennedy were created with random newspaper clippings. The results were astonishing. There was no use of pencil or ink, as each line and shade was a piece of newspaper.

First Lady Jackie Kennedy

Newsclip Collage (21″ H x 20″ W)

Mother Teresa

Newsclip Collage (21" H x 20" W)

This was the first portrait where Sorcar used newspaper clippings relevant to the subject. The portrait of Mother Teresa was done with Bengali newspaper pieces about her. They were imported from Kolkata (formerly Calcutta), India, where she first started her charity order. "For shades, I searched several newspapers to find flaws in ink impressions. The font size, ink darkness, quality of the print, and even the color of the actual newsprint had a significant role in creating the relief and 3-D effect," explains Sorcar.

Mother Teresa

Newsclip Collage (21″ H x 20″ W)

This portrait was done exclusively with internet clippings. Various articles from many sites were used to help convey Mother Teresa's international deeds.

Princess Diana

Newsclip Collage (21" H x 20" W)

Collage of Peoples' Princess Diana with news clippings about her from newspapers, as well as internet publishings.

Wellington Webb

Newsclip Collage (29.5" H x 26.5" W)

Successful mission rips through criticism. During the time of Denver International Airport's construction, Wellington Webb was Denver's first African-American mayor. He inherited the project from the previous mayor and was subject to sharp criticism for its increasing costs. Despite all of the opposition, Webb emerged as a popular mayor when the beautiful airport was completed, proving to be one of the most successful airports in the world.

President Clinton and the 1996 Election

Newsclip Collage (42" H x 40" W)

Relevant news clippings of seven months prior to the 1996 Presidential election were saved in making this portrait. The clippings outline the story of the campaign race between Bill Clinton, Robert Dole and Ross Perot. The last piece of newspaper used was the day after the election, when the results were announced.

THE DENVER POST

Sunny, Milder
High 66, Low 42
Complete weather, 12B

Voice of the Rocky Mountain Empire • 25¢ — May vary outside metro Denver

ART SHOW PICK

October 18, 1996

FRIDAY

Portraits of newsmakers, including Mother Teresa, left, and Wellington Webb, made by P.C. 'Manick' Sorcar from newspaper clippings about the newsmakers are among works on view at Foothills Art Center, 809 15th St., Golden. 'Images of India' and two other exhibits, 'Quiet Pride' and 'Landscapes West' are open through Oct. 27. Call 279-3922 for more information.

Artist Displays Wizardry at Foothills

"Manick Sorcar, a lighting engineer and artist from Golden, specializes in feats that will astound... Taking on sleight of hand few would attempt, the artist has created portraits of Asian and American newsmakers, using as his medium—newspapers."

Jefferson County Transcript
USA
October 11, 1996

"Less is more: The Foothills Art Center, known for its blockbuster juried watermedia and sculpture shows, takes a respite from the sprawl by presenting a trio of intriguing little shows... The works in Images of India, created by Manick Sorcar, appear at first sight to be simple portraits, painted in traditional Indian style, of famous figures from Gandhi to John and Jackie Kennedy. But a closer gander reveals the unusual materials used, including rice grains, colored spices and crumpled newspapers, to arrange collages as detailed as a Native American sand painting."

Westword newspaper
USA
October 3, 1996

Method Behind the News Art

Creating the newsclip collage was painstaking, but Sorcar enjoyed perfecting the minute details of each portrait. First, he drew a pencil sketch of the person. Then he meticulously pasted tiny bits of newspaper clippings on the contours of the face. It was a challenge because as the lines got covered, there was no reference. He had to rely on his imagination to complete the image. But Sorcar carefully captured every detail of the person's face in his mind, then tried to recapture it with an appropriate newspaper clip; whether it was Diana's *kohled* eyes, the wrinkles on Mother Teresa's face, or the creases near Clinton's eyes. It was like piecing together a jigsaw puzzle.

(top) **"Art Show Pick"** by *The Denver Post*, October 18, 1996. The art exhibition was held at the historic Foothills Art Center in Golden, Colorado, USA, for the entire month of October.

49

The Drummer Lady

Acrylic on tile (21" H x 20" W)

Tile Art

   One of Sorcar's art exhibitions was dedicated to stone art based on statuettes found in the Sun Temple of Khajuraho, cave art of Ellora and Ajanta, India. He used the technique of pointillism, a series of strategically placed dots, in painting the reliefs on the stone slabs. This gave the paintings the three-dimensional look that was associated with the statuettes.

Tree Goddess

Acrylic on tile (21″ H x 10″ W)

Nataraja (Shiva)

Acrylic on tile (each 21" H x 20" W)

Brahma-Vishnu-Maheshwara

Acrylic on tile (each 21" H x 20" W)

Amorous Couple

Acrylic on tile (each 21" H x 20" W)

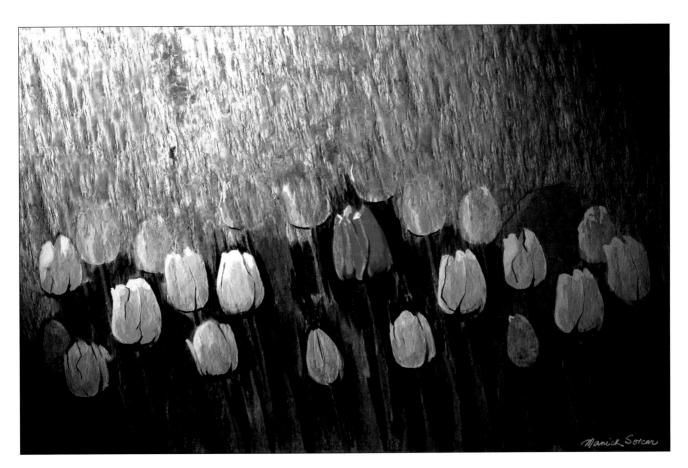

Tulips

Acrylic on slate (21″ H x 32″ W)

Slate Art

Sorcar enjoyed painting soft subjects such as flowers and leaves on hard surfaces, which was the theme of a series of artwork he did on slates. "The slates are porous—they quickly absorbed the paint, leaving only a trace of the color." He enjoyed showing this vanishing act of the flowers in the rock.

Pond Blooms

Acrylic on slates (26″ H x 24.5″ W)

Fall Color

Acrylic on slate (21″ H x 20″ W)

Maple leaves of Fall against rock. This piece of acrylic painting on slate was auctioned on-air at KRMA-TV (PBS) the popular educational channel, for raising funds.

Priest King from Mohenjodaro

Acrylic on slate (21" H x 20" W)

While using hard surface as his canvas, Sorcar came up with another idea for a new series of art. It was his dream series, glorifying the rich history of India. The rugged surface of the slates reminded him of the Indus Valley Civilization (2600 B.C.) findings. And so, a whole new series of painting was born, based on this ancient, old civilization, which flourished in the vast river plains and adjacent regions which are now Pakistan and western India. The archaeologists discovered many statuettes, seals and crafts of the old civilization. These discoveries had a significant impact on Sorcar's art, as he re-introduced these ancient icons in a unique form as paintings on slates. Even the selection of the slate had a major significance in the overall presentation. For instance, the crack in the slate above reflects the cracks in the original statuettes.

A Seal from Harappa

Acrylic on slate (21″ H x 20″ W)

Terra - cotta Figurine from Harappa

Acrylic on slate (21″ H x 20″ W)

Buddha

Acrylic on slate (21″ H x 20″ W)

Shringar

Tile Collage (26.5" H x 18.5" W)

Tile Collage Art

In early 2000, Sorcar introduced another type of art medium: Tile Collage. Synthetic floor tiles of different colors were cut to precision and glued on a larger piece of tile. For this particular picture, ornaments were touched up with acrylic paints.

Ganesha

Tile Collage (41.25″ H x 36.5″ W)

Tile collage of the Hindu God of prosperity and wisdom.

Dhaki (the Drummer)

Tile Collage (26.5" H x 18.5" W)

"Dhaki" is the Bengali word for the drummer who plays the drum during "Durga Puja," the auspicious day of homage to Goddess Durga. It is one of the biggest Hindu festivals of India.

Gautama Buddha

Tile Collage (49.5″ H x 41.5″ W)

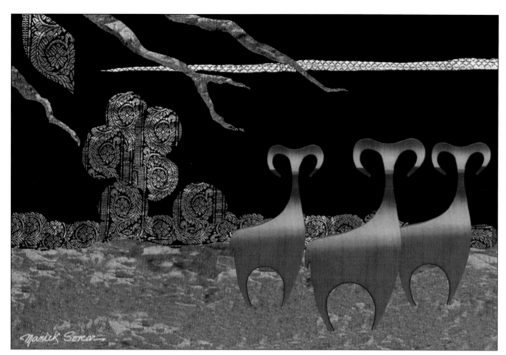

Alert

Digital Art (16″ H x 24″ W) (Individual)
(16″ H x 72″ W) (Panoramic)

Digital Art

For the first time, Sorcar combined his traditional art with computer technology to create striking art in digital media, using the computer screen as the canvas. It launched a new series of digital art by Sorcar.

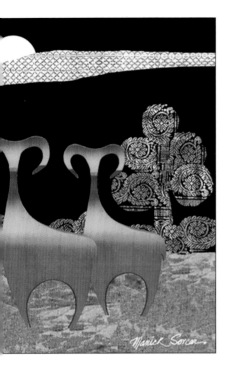
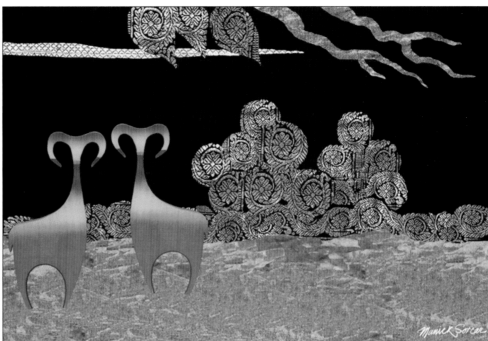

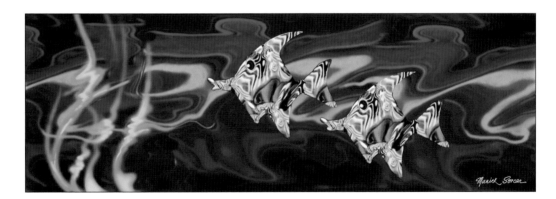

Under Deep Water

Digital Art (16″ H x 50″ W)

(top) A contemporary take on a panoramic view of animals at night.
(bottom) Fish in the deep blue ocean.

Boatman in Sunset

Digital Art (12" H x 30" W)

(top) The silhouette of a boatman was a typical scene that Sorcar had witnessed along the Ganges river in Benares, India during his electrical engineering student days. A realistic rendition with a digital brush.

Manick Sorcar

Colors in Motion

Digital Art (12" H x 18" W)

(top) Sorcar's imagination flies with the butterfly, creating a motion-blur in the painting. The wings are adorned with beautiful Indian motifs. "I wanted to fly with the butterfly and capture its image with my mind's camera."

Stare at the Sky

Digital Art (24" H x 41" W)

Purple Blooms

Digital Art (24" H x 41" W)

The digital brush and over a million different color options on the computer opened up endless possibilities. Each of Sorcar's creations in this medium was refreshing and different from anything he had done before. "They light up my room with smiles," was a comment from one of his dedicated customers who had purchased much of Sorcar's artwork.

Smiling Bunch

Digital Art (33″ H x 30″ W)

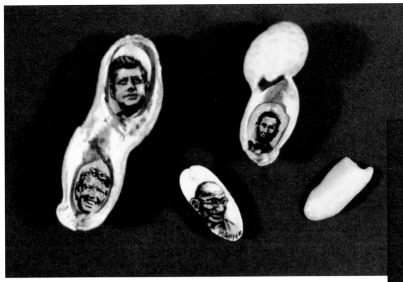

The Peanut Gallery

Peanut art

Artist: Manick Sorcar

Grain of History

Rice grain art

"They are different than anything else you have seen and exclusively of his own. Each piece is a work of magic!"

Carol Dickinson
Former Executive Director/ Curator of Foothills Art Center
Golden, Colorado, USA

Assorted Art

Somewhere inside the serious artist was a fun-loving and nutty artist who saw art even in the mundane. By choosing offbeat canvases such as grains of rice and peanuts, Sorcar showed that art can be expressed on virtually any canvas.

In the late-70's, he painted a portrait of Jimmy Carter on half of a peanut. Appropriate indeed, as Carter was a peanut farmer. Sorcar's idea was to paint Rosalyn Carter on the other half of the peanut and then present the two to the Carters. But, "Rosalyn's face was hard to draw," explains Sorcar. "I spent over 8 hours to paint it and when finished, I left it on the table to take a short break. When I returned, Jimmy Carter was still there, but Rosalyn's peanut was gone—like magic. I desperately looked for it everywhere. Soon I found out who the magician was—it was my one year-old daughter, who was still chomping on it."

Carter was not lonely for long. Soon there were portraits of many other world leaders including Abraham Lincoln, John F. Kennedy, Jackie Kennedy, Mahatma Gandhi and more. "For painting on a grain of rice, I used a magnifying glass and a special brush with two hairs, which was still too thick for the tiny surface. One hair wouldn't even pick up ink! It was a challenge. I could only work in two-hour increments before getting a severe headache."

These pieces are just as unique as the materials used for each composition.

Ganesha

Spice painting (26" H x 20" W)

Ingredients:

Background:	Mustard seeds, lentils, barley
Floor:	Fennel seeds
Plate:	Fenugreeks
Food:	Barley
Body:	Garlic, cumin seeds
Hair:	Onion seeds
Ornaments:	Lentils, mustard seeds, fennel seeds
Eyes/Eyebrows:	Cumin seeds, onion seeds
Ears:	Paprika, garlic
Mouse:	Cinnamon grounds

One of Sorcar's earlier artwork used only seeds and spices to create an exquisite composition. "The good thing about this kind of art is that if you don't like it, you eat it," says Sorcar.

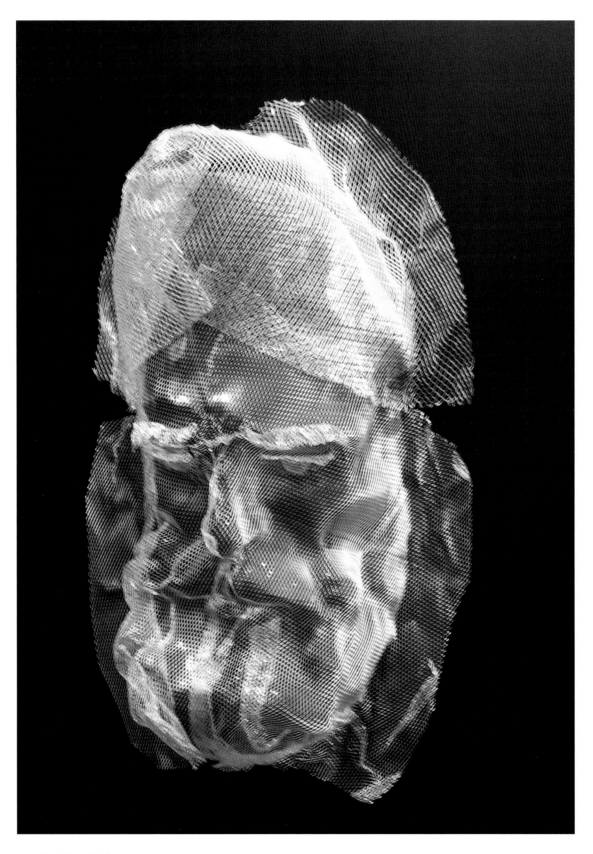

Old Man

Chicken wire sculpture (26″ H x 20″ W)

Brick on Brick

Acrylic on brick slices (38" H x 20" W)

A trip to India had prompted Sorcar to do a very special painting of a child worker. Dust had fallen from the bricks and covered almost all of the child's body, all except the faint smile on his face.

This was the beginning of a series of paintings which Sorcar started in early 2000, combining delicate subjects with rough, textured surfaces, such as bricks and tiles. This particular piece was drawn with acrylic paint on brick slices.

Relief Work in an Alcove

Acrylic on wood & decor (70" H x 72" W)

(top) A unique piece of artwork that is showcased in an alcove at Sorcar's residence. "I designed it specifically for that location," says Sorcar, "each piece was first cut out of plywood. It was then covered with colored papier-mâché for texture. The floral art was then painted with acrylic."

Love

Caulking art (6′ H x 9′ W)

Conversation

Acrylic on foamboard (6″ H x 10″ W)

(top) The headboard of the king-size bed in the master bedroom is an artwork created by Sorcar. Precision-cut tiles and caulked contours are accented by LED lighting.
(bottom) Symmetry in art.

Street Musicians

Styrofoam sculpture (6' H x 6.5' W)

(top left) "Street Musicians" on a Styrofoam relief. Layers of industrial-grade Styrofoam sheets are glued together and then carved with a hobby knife to produce the life-size sculpture.
(bottom left) Man with flute.
(right) Drummer Lady.

"কেট্রিনায় সপরিবারে"
Artist: MANICK SORCAR

Goddess Durga,

Acrylic on foamboard (8' H x 11' W)

"At Katrina With the Whole Family"

In the year 2005, Sorcar painted the image of Goddess Durga in a new avatar. Goddess Durga in Hindu mythology symbolizes good over evil. The Hindus believe that she visits once every year with her family and a continuous ten days are celebrated to welcome her. This was the year when hurricane Katrina had devastated New Orleans, Louisiana, USA, and the neighboring areas. In this image, Goddess Durga is carrying her son, baby Ganesha, in her arms in deep waters with her children. She is here to share the grief and to bring hope, symbolized by the rainbow.

Inspiration.

Color pencils on a piece of paper (11" H x 8.5" W)

   This piece of art represents Shikha's coming into Manick Sorcar's life. Drawn on a piece of paper, it is still mounted on the wall, facing his work station in the studio. "She faded into my life from nowhere and filled it with vibrant color," says Sorcar. Apart from being an ideal wife and mother to his two daughters, Shikha is an inseparable companion and the main source of inspiration for all of Sorcar's activities. They celebrated their 25th wedding anniversary in 1999.

Various Art Exhibitions

A few select images of Sorcar's art exhibitions that started from his college days at the University of Washington, Seattle, USA.

Sorcar Residence

Art in Architecture

Sorcar's 7,800 square-foot custom-made home is an architectural masterpiece. With a touch of architecture of the Moghul period, Sorcar designed it like a "mini-India" where he can retire to at the end of the day. *The Rocky Mountain News* of Denver, Colorado, USA, called it a "Shrine to Indian Culture." The magnificent house showcases Sorcar's multi-media art, ranging from traditional water paint on paper, acrylic on raw-silk, straw-paper and bamboo trays to tile paintings, newspaper collages, oil-based markers on newsprint, miniature paintings with Indian ink, clay and Styrofoam sculptures to caulking artwork on a wall covered with floor tiles.

(top) The front entryway that leads into the beautiful Sorcar residence.
(bottom) The Sorcar residence emitting a magical aura during the evening.

"Eastern Star: Lakeshore Home is Shrine to Indian Culture" was the heading of the Home Front section of *The Rocky Mountain News*—the oldest and immensely popular newspaper of Colorado, which dedicated two full color pages to the Sorcar residence.

"On weekdays, Manick Sorcar lives the quintessential fast-paced life of a businessman, pitching his company's electrical engineering services to multi-million dollar clients. But evenings and weekends, he steps into a peaceful haven and leaves the corporate world far behind. Sorcar, a native of Calcutta, goes home to modern India without ever leaving Colorado. To recharge, he kicks off his shoes at the door of the two-story stucco home he designed on Hyatt Lake in Arvada. He steps into the cool, marble-tiled foyer and immerses himself in his culture. With his wife, Shikha, and their daughters, Piya and Payal, he experiences his native country's languages, dress, paintings, music and cuisine."

Betsy Lehndorff
Rocky Mountain News
USA
August 18, 2001

(top) The 22-foot high octagonal great room is defined by arched windows with a stunning view of the Hyatt lake in Arvada, Colorado, USA. The furnishings and decor reflect Indian art in every corner.

(top & bottom) The bathroom is designed like an Indian portico with columns that separate it from the master bedroom. The perimeter walls are covered with multi-layered mirrors of different shades, all cut as mountains at the top. Glass block walls are tastefully located around the bathroom and they reflect on the mirrors to give an illusion of reflecting water.

(top) The Master Bedroom is an exquisite work of art, as the rest of the house.

(bottom left) Lighting of contrasting era and elegance. Curtain of candle holder near a glass-block wall illuminated with fibre-optics.

(bottom right) Splash of color through glass block.

The architecture of Sorcar was of great interest to Betsy Lehndorff, the writer of the article, who researched more about Indian architecture and wrote:

"If you are interested in finding out more about the origins of Indian architecture, take a look at the *Indian-Decoration—Interiors-Design* by author-photographer Henry Wilson. Published by Watson-Guptill, the $40 book with 340 illustrations arrives at bookstores this month. Wilson's photographs of village and city homes help explain the roots of Manick Sorcar's architecture.

The book shows many of the repetitive arches within arches that inspired the facade of Sorcar's house. Pierced wooden or marble screens with elaborate carvings in windows deflect the sun's heat and provide privacy, much as Sorcar's glass blocks do."

Betsy Lehndorff
Rocky Mountain News
USA
August 18, 2001

(top) A view of the back of the Sorcar home.
(bottom) A stunning view of the backyard, overlooking Hyatt Lake.

Patrons of Denver Art Museum visit Sorcar Residence

The residence completely decorated with Sorcar's own India-motif artwork was an attraction not only to the public, but also to the Asian Art Association (AAA) of the Denver Art Museum. Twenty-two patrons of the association, along with its President and Curator, visited the residence for a personal experience of the unique artwork, on September 25, 2001.

(top) Sorcar and his wife, Shikha and their daughters, Piya and Payal, with Elizabeth Shwayder, President of the Asian Art Association.
(bottom left) Patrons of the Asian Art Association admire Sorcar's artwork at his residence in Arvada, Colorado.
(bottom right) Sorcar with Elizabeth Shwayder and Ronald Otsuka, Curator of the Asian Art Association of the Denver Art Museum.

(top) A stunning, two-story chandelier with illuminated links of various streams in length runs through the core of the round staircase. The glittering light gives a 'halo' effect, making it a center of attraction. The chandelier, adorned with a cluster of miniature bulbs that were rated for 40,000 hours, was designed by Sorcar.

(bottom) Patrons of the Asian Art Association of the Denver Art Museum admire the chandelier.

ACT THREE:
Cartoonist

The mischief of the peanut portraits revealed the child in Manick Sorcar. He realized that he could combine humor with art to tell a story, and decided the best medium for this combination was cartoons—which he regards as simply another form of art. In his own words, "I was simply amused and intrigued by the teething troubles of the Indian immigrants, who were straddling two cultures. I thought the best way of sharing and recording our stories was through cartoons." And just like that, Sorcar decided to draw cartoons.

Sorcar's journey as a cartoonist began in the 70's through a community newspaper called Samachar, for the Indian community in Colorado. This was the perfect platform for his outrageously funny cartoons which captured the dilemma of the immigrant Indian in the United States. Sorcar's take on the colorful experiences of an immigrant struck a chord with the readers—both Indian and non-Indian. His first batch of cartoons published in Samachar created a wave through the community, tapping into common experiences to which all immigrants could relate.

The cartoons were like laughter-therapy for the immigrants challenged by inhabiting two worlds at the same time. Sorcar drew from everyday life experiences—going to the grocery store, traveling, and attending parties—and filtered them through a comic lens. The Sorcartoons became a favorite of the American and Indian media.

As the oldest Indo-American newspaper, India Abroad aptly said, Sorcar's cartoons "chronicles through caricatures the foibles and idiosyncrasies of Indian immigrants on a tightrope walk between the two lifestyles." Sorcartoons became a regular feature of popular newspapers and magazines such as India Abroad, The Link, India West, India Tribune and so on. Besides highlighting the comic side of Sorcar, these cartoons also documented the experiences of first generation immigrants to America. Future generations are able to look back at these cartoons to laugh and marvel at the experiences of their forefathers who managed to find an identity with little support and left a rich legacy for their descendants.

Starting with only $8 in his pocket, and faced with all the challenges of acclimating to a new society while raising a family in the United States, here is the life of an immigrant as seen through "Sorcartoons."

WE ENJOY HAVING YOU AS OUR FOREIGN STUDENT, APPRECIATE YOUR POLITENESS... BUT PLEASE, CALL ME TOM, NOT UNCLE

SO, YOU ARE AN INDIAN, EH! ... WHAT TRIBE?

"Electrical engineer of Denver, Colorado, and son of the Late P.C. Sorcar, India's legendary magician, Manick Sorcar is undoubtedly a top expresser of the U.S. Indian immigrant experience. His illustrations, touching the heart of cultural integration challenges, are compiled in two volumes—*The Melting Pot, Indians in America*, and *Spices in the Melting Pot*."

Hinduism Today
USA
August, 1998

"YES OPERATOR... MY NAME IS
RAMBHAROSA... "R" AS IN RUDRAMURTHY,
"A" AS IN AGARBATTI, "M" AS IN MANMOHAN
"B" AS IN ..."

"I CAN'T PRONOUNCE YOUR NAME
BUT I CAN SEE IT IS THERE"

"BACK IN THE SCHOOL DAYS,
I KNEW ANOTHER CIVIL ENGINEER
FROM INDIA ... DO YOU KNOW HIM ?"

YOU GUYS IN INDIA MUST
BE LUCKY... NO AIR POLLUTION
WITH ELEPHANTS...

"BOTH OF US GREW UP IN CALCUTTA WITHOUT ANY HELP FROM MOTHER TERESA"

HERE IT IS! A DIET GHEE JUST FOR YOU... I MADE IT WITH ONLY 2% FAT MILK!!

HOW MUCH IS THE CAULIFLOWER WITHOUT THE LEAVES?

.. AND THIS'S MY LONG-TIME NEIGHBOR, ENGINEER-CARTOONIST FROM INDIA, MANNIX SOCCER ..

IF THIS IS WHAT YOU CALL
"ENJOYING LIFE" — THEN WHAT WAS WRONG
WITH OUR VILLAGE JHUMRITALAIA?

I NEITHER UNDERSTAND YOUR
DOCTOR'S HANDWRITING, NOR HIS
ACCENT — WHAT'RE YOUR SYMPTOMS?

Cartoonist Offers a 'Manick' View Of Indian Life in America

By ROB SHUBOW

Denver, Colo. — "When in Rome, do as the Romans do" is an old adage which may translate these days into "when you're an Indian in America, be an American Indian — you'll be taken for one anyway." At least that's part of the message offered by Manick (otherwise known as Prafulla C. Sorcar), a wry observer of Indian emigrant life, who makes his "sorcar-stic" comments through the medium of cartoons.

He may be called Manick, but he certainly is not depressive — at least his cartoons aren't — but adept at finding humor even in the most alienating or frustrating of circumstances. And for strangers in a strange land, as Indians here often find themselves, such circumstances are not unusual.

Manick, an engineer by profession ("of course I'm an engineer," his cartoon hero would say, "I'm from India, aren't I?") has just published a collection of his satirical sketchings entitled The Melting Pot: Indians in America.

Much of his humor emerges from his own daily experiences, as when an engineering colleague told him he knew immediately from his accent that he was Indian — and then pro-

Prafulla C. [Manick] Sorcar, cartoonist and engineer: "Life has been funny."

ceeded to ask him what tribe . .or the time he was asked if his native language was 'Indiana.'

But most of his inspirations come from attending Indian parties here, observing the foibles of his fellow emigrants and hearing their stories. He feels that his cartoons serve the therapeutic function of letting others know that they are not suffering alone, but that many Indians face the same dilemmas and compromises — and often find American society ridiculous for the same reasons. Sorcar's drawings thus validate a world view which might otherwise seem mad.

Of course, Sorcar's of

movie — only one theatre is empty and the other holds a packed house. The only difference is a poster at the front door of the second one advertising "free food & snacks after show."

Other aspects of life which come under Manick's impish scrutiny include the problems of raising children here, of dealing with customs officials and other bureaucrats, and socializing with American friends. "Life has been so funny," says India-West, "th a shortage

What is time, for ties keep — and second obligati

Krishna disciple, finding such culture-jumping often irrational and escapist.

Indian behavior at public gatherings likewise comes under attack from his sharp pen, particularly in the sketch depicting

claimed author of several texts used by engineers and students worldwide. The idea for his first book — entitl Lighting D

His seco ing Lighti

"Much of his humor emerges from his own experiences... but most of his inspirations come from attending Indian parties here, observing the foibles of his fellow immigrants and hearing their stories. He feels that his cartoons serve the therapeutic function of letting others know that they are not suffering alone, but that many Indians face the same dilemmas and compromises—and often find American society ridiculous for the same reasons. Sorcar's drawings thus validate a world view which might otherwise seem mad."

Rob Shubow
India West
USA
June 25, 1982

"...TAKE A SMALL CAN OF *RICOTTA* CHEESE AND MIX WITH A *FISTFULL* OF FLOUR.... ADD TWO *FINGER-DIP* OF GHEE WITH ONE *PINCH* OF SALT.... FRY UNTIL COLOR IS *NUTTY*...THEN SOAK INTO A *STRING-THICK* OF SYRUP..."

WOULD YOU CONSIDER SELLING THE REST OF THE HOUSE?

" I THOUGHT YOU MIGHT LIKE TO TRY SOMETHING NEW ...THIS'S CALLED ICE CREAM"

"IT'S EASY, REMEMBER ?
TUCK, WRAP, PLEAT-PLEAT-PLEAT,
TUCK & DONE !!"

"SOME HABITS WILL NEVER CHANGE..
..LIKE WHEN THEY CALL INDIA !"

"IT'S 'TU CHEEZ BADI HAI MUSTA
MUSTA'.... NOT 'TWO CHEESE
BURRITOS MUSTARD MUSTARD' "

"AH! I FINALLY FOUND SOMETHING
ABSOLUTELY AMERICAN ! "

© MANICK SORCAR

American Guru

"DO YOU HAVE ANYTHING ELSE VALUABLE TO DECLARE OTHER THAN FOUR SUITCASES OF DIAPERS?"

"SORRY, NO INDIAN FILMS ALLOWED.. ...THIS IS ASIAN FILM FESTIVAL"

IT'S O.K. DEAR, THEY SAID THESE ARE ALL COOKED IN CHOLESTEROL-FREE OIL

"BUT THESE ARE STANDARD SUITCASES THAT MEASURE WELL UNDER 62 INCHES ... WHEN EMPTY"

"...AND THIS IS 'LACHHMI', IN AMERICAN, IT MEANS A TAX DEDUCTION"

"IGNORE MY PARENTS, THEY DON'T EVEN KNOW THE MEANING OF A SLUMBER PARTY"

THERE! JUST THE RIGHT SIZE ... FOR THE NEXT FOUR YEARS ...

I BET OUR ACTORS CAN BEAT UP
ANY OF YOUR ACTORS!

NO, LORD GANESH DOESN'T WANT IT; FINISH YOUR MILK!

" TRY AGAIN SON... IT'S SEETA RAM , NOT CD-ROM "

GUESS WHAT! RAVI SPOKE HIS FIRST WORD TODAY— "COKE"

..AND THAT'S MUMMY WITH HER WEDDING RING...SHE PUT IT ON HER NOSE 'CAUSE SHE HAD A SORE FINGER..

YOU KNOW, USA TRULY IS A MELTING POT... MY DAUGHTER JUST GOT ENGAGED TO A SOUTH INDIAN!

"I'LL NEVER MARRY ANYONE FROM INDIA – THEY ALL HAVE DAD'S ACCENT!"

BEFORE YOU TAKE MY DAUGHTER OUT, LET ME ASK YOU A FEW QUESTIONS.
– WHAT DOES YOUR FATHER DO? °°°

SORRY DAD, WE COULDN'T TAKE YOU WITH US TO RAJU'S HOME... IT'S AN ADULT PARTY.

"...AND I DON'T KNOW WHY THEY CALL IT A 'SARI'... IT SHOULD BE 'SORRY'!"

"THE ONLY TIME I GET A CHANCE TO DANCE WITH MY HUSBAND IS AT THE HARE KRSNA TEMPLE... AND YOU?"

Kolkata UNPLUGGED

Laugh your art out

Manick Sorcar has etched Bengali identity in popular animation and cartoons in the West. Mathures Paul reads between panels

"I'LL NEVER MARRY ANYONE FROM INDIA – THEY ALL HAVE DAD'S ACCENT!"

YOU are well up on outsourcing of cartoons and the evergreen comic book characters produced by the West. As far as Bengali cartoons are concerned, Narayan Debnath has no competition. But what about Bengali animation? The ones making it to the market are not up to the mark and are, to a good extent, amateurish.

Manick Sorcar or Prafulla C Sorcar is an electrical engineer from Bengal who is currently settled in Colorado. He is a frequent flyer to India and has to his credit a number of animation titles. Education-wise, he is an engineer and is presently CEO/president of Sorcar Engineering (formerly Butterweck-Sorcar Engineering, Inc.), an electrical engineering firm in Denver that he and his former partner, late Howard Butterweck, started in 1974.

"But inside, I am all artist. I have

been an artist ever since I was a young child. When my father noticed my simultaneous interest in art and science, he encouraged me to paint his scenes and create lighting designs for his stage sets, which eventually inspired me to become an electrical engineer. But I could not give up my love for the arts. Cartooning is only a small segment of my wide interest in various forms of art, which took serious shape after I moved to the United States and began to notice the idiosyncrasies of my fellow Indians living in America on a tightrope between two lifestyles. So many comical things were happening daily basis. I wanted to capture them and share them with f generations of Indian an inkling of the of their forebea

ever, it is just the opposite. Ironically, it is perfectly appropriate, at the same dinner table, to loudly blow your nose into a tissue paper in front of all the guests cartoons serve two prime es. The first is, of c smile to the reader second is to prov function to le the rea

children (199

"Manick Sorcar has etched Bengali identity in popular animation and cartoons in the West."

Mathures Paul
The Statesman
Kolkata Unplugged Section
April 3, 2006

" INDIAN, AMERICAN, CANADIAN, ITALIAN — WE DON'T CARE WHO YOU MARRY — SO LONG AS HE IS A BRAHMIN! "

" 'SUE-LUCK-SHAUNA-ANJIE-LEE' ? WHAT A LOVELY NAME! WHICH ONE I SHOULD CALL YOU ? "

" ...AND IT'S OUR CUSTOM IF SHE GOES OUT ON A DATE — **MOTHER GOES WITH HER!** "

" ...EVERY OTHER YEAR THE GURU APPEARS IN USA FROM THIN AIR TO GIVE HIS BLESSINGS ... AND TO RENEW HIS GREEN CARD "

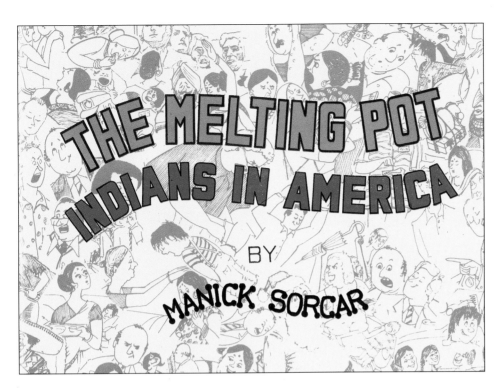

Sorcartoons are compiled in two popular books. The books were dedicated to "the future generation of Indians in America: An inkling of the teething troubles of their forebears." The books are available at libraries, bookstores, on-line stores, and Sorcar's website: www.manicksorcar.com

(top) Cover of The Melting Pot: Indians in America.
(bottom) Cover of Spices in the Melting Pot.

ACT FOUR:
Animator

The metamorphosis of Sorcar's cartoons to animation was a journey which sprung from a strong personal desire. In the 1980's, Sorcar and his wife Shikha wanted to help their U.S.-born daughters learn more about their native culture. It broke their hearts that their daughters only spoke in English and could not communicate with their grandparents and family in India.

Sorcar's dream was to create a unique, culturally stimulating work that would also engage his daughters, Piya (then 8) and Payal (then 5). Once again, he turned to art to express his desires and chose music and animation as a form of education. He wanted to make learning fun and wrote music and Bengali lyrics to which they could sing and dance. To help them learn about Indian culture, Sorcar produced and directed children's videos in which his daughters would act with animated characters. During the creative process, his daughters asked him many questions about their cultural roots. It was a way for the family to learn together and at the same time share their works of art with the rest of the world.

The title of the first video production was East Meets West, and it was a smash hit with the local channels. The big breakthrough, however, came in the early 90's when he produced his first major animation film for children, combined with live action: "Deepa and Rupa: A Fairy Tale from India." From cartoons, animation was a natural creative leap for Sorcar. To him, it was as simple as "cartoons in motion." He selected humorous and memorable characters from Indian folk tales and drew them on an 11" x 17" layout. Until the emergence of personal computers, each of the hundreds of background scenes was painstakingly drawn on paper, the same method used in Walt Disney's classic films. Using legends and folk stories from Indian culture such as The Panchatantra, he taught his daughters timeless Indian values, traditions and morals, in a most engaging way. Elaborate village settings in Bengal and characters in their local costumes, took the Western audience to rural India.

Sorcar reveled in his new avatar as an animator. What started at home as a small family education project soon became a national phenomenon in bridging East and West. His films won international acclaim and awards, were used in schools and studied in universities, and became popular television programs. It's no surprise that for the 16th year in a row, Sorcar's animation have been telecast on the Rocky Mountain PBS channels of Colorado, USA.

Inspired by this success, Sorcar went on to single-handedly produce five full-scale animation films. These films had a refreshing quality and warmth about them that is often lacking in slick, big-budget films.. After experiencing so much success from bringing legendary Indian fairy tales to life, in the end he created his own fairy tale.

"Santa Claus"
Lyrics/Tune by
Manick Sorcar

(Original song in Bengali.
Translated in English.)

"Santa Claus come with me to India
Let me introduce you
To the 'Champa brothers'
And lovely sister Parul too

It's the land of water-fairies
And birds on many a golden tree
But if the boogey-man ever gets you
I promise I'll make you free

In the jungle with Mr. Lion and uncle Tiger
There will also be Rudolph deer
He will play with sister Shakuntala
Who knows no violence, just love and tender care

I'll decorate the floors to welcome you,
And leave a lot of sweets, just for you,
When the whole village falls asleep,
Leave us a toy, will you, please?"

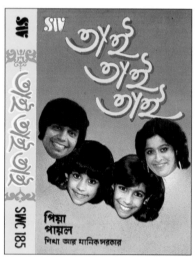

"Magical music of Manick Sorcar... *Chhucho Kattaar Biye*
(Wedding of the Mole Leader) indeed gets the children and
even their parents excited, as the songs of Piya and Payal
magically take the listeners to Disneyland."

Aaj Kaal
India
July 1986

Sorcar's Music

(top left) Manufactured by CBS Records, USA, and released in 1984, *Santa Claus* & *Ajagar* (Python) were sung
by his daughters Piya (then 8) and Payal (then 5). Piya received the First Prize for her song *Santa Claus* at the
Stars of Tomorrow contest sponsored by the Kiwanis International Club.
(top right) Image of Sorcar's second record, *Chhucho Kattaar Biye* (Wedding of the Mole Leader) in 1986. This
45 RPM album was recorded by SoundWing Company of India.
(bottom) Sorcar's two cassettes, *Chhucho Kattaar Biye* (Wedding of the Mole Leader) released in 1986, and *Tai,
Tai, Tai* (Clap, Clap, Clap) released in 1987, both distributed by SoundWing Company of India.

"In the Sweet Morning"
Lyrics/Tune
Manick Sorcar

(Original song in Bengali.
Translated in English.)

"In the sweet morning
In the cool breeze
Pretty butterflies fly around
In the smiling sunshine

The black cow says moo-moo-moo
The rooster says koo-ke-koo
Little birdie says too-too-too
But the silly donkey just looks at you

The little duckling is sad
She was up all night,
Her mama scolded her
So she didn't eat her milk and rice
She just yawns and yawns
Will doze off any time

The little kid with round eyes
Wobbles and walks behind his mama
He stops to smell the grass
But, wait! A naughty cricket!
Oh run, run, run!! What a drama!"

(top left) The popular children's songs of Piya & Payal were re-released on CD in 2006.
(top right) Piya and Payal at the recording studio in the U.S. during rehearsal in 1984.
(bottom) Sorcar and his daughters during a song rehearsal at the same studio.

Two Songs From the East

This was Manick Sorcar's first animation (1985), *Two Children's Songs From the East*. It contained two of his songs, "Santa Claus," and, "In the Sweet Morning," each having live action with animation. All of the artwork was hand-drawn by Sorcar himself. In "Santa Claus," a little girl takes Santa Claus to India, bridging the two cultures together. In "In the Sweet Morning," another girl goes inside her own artwork and interacts with her painted friends. These songs were sung by Sorcar's daughters Piya, then 8, and Payal, then 5. They were also telecast on Doordarshan—the television broadcasting network of the Government of India.

(top) A little girl, played by Piya Sorcar, with Santa Claus.
(middle & bottom) Payal Sorcar singing and dancing with her animal friends inside her drawing.

East Meets West

The success with his own children was a great inspiration for Sorcar to widen the cultural bridge to a larger audience. In 1986 he brought art, music and animation together into one platform through his videos based in rural Bengal. The first opportunity to show his unique work was with American CableVision of Colorado, USA, where *East Meets West*, a half-hour children's program was shown. Sorcar explained the theme of each song written by him, while his daughters sang, danced and interacted with his art and animation.

The entire background was hand-painted while the animated characters were a combination of hand-painted pictures and computer imaging. The integration to the live action was done at the American CableVision studio.

The half-hour program was a hit within the U.S. and was aired several times. The popular demand inspired Sorcar to produce a sequel the following year, titled *East Meets West II*, with new songs and animation.

(top) Sorcar was interviewed by American CableVision prior to the showing of each episode of *East Meets West*.
(bottom) Payal Sorcar and Mike Potter, the Production Coordinator of American CableVision, during the filming of one of the songs from *East Meets West*, at the studio of American Cablevision.

Deepa & Rupa: A Fairy Tale From India

   This was Manick Sorcar's first major, full-scale children's film that blended live action with animation. Sorcar picked a simple, popular fairy tale based in Bengal. He made the live characters interact seamlessly with animated characters such as a horse, banyan tree, clouds and a cow. The film resonated with a wide variety of audiences—parents, children, teachers and the media. It was a result of countless hours in the night and weekends for three years (1988-1990). The half-hour film taught essential Indian values such as respecting mother nature in a wonderfully subtle way. According to *The Denver Post*, "television is not always the sterile, corporate, slick medium we love to knock. Occasionally, a home-grown, family project (*Deepa & Rupa*), slips through and humanizes the machine." The three-year labor of love became a legend forever.

   (top) Deepa Reddy, left, and Piya Sorcar as two stepsisters in a scene from *Deepa & Rupa*.

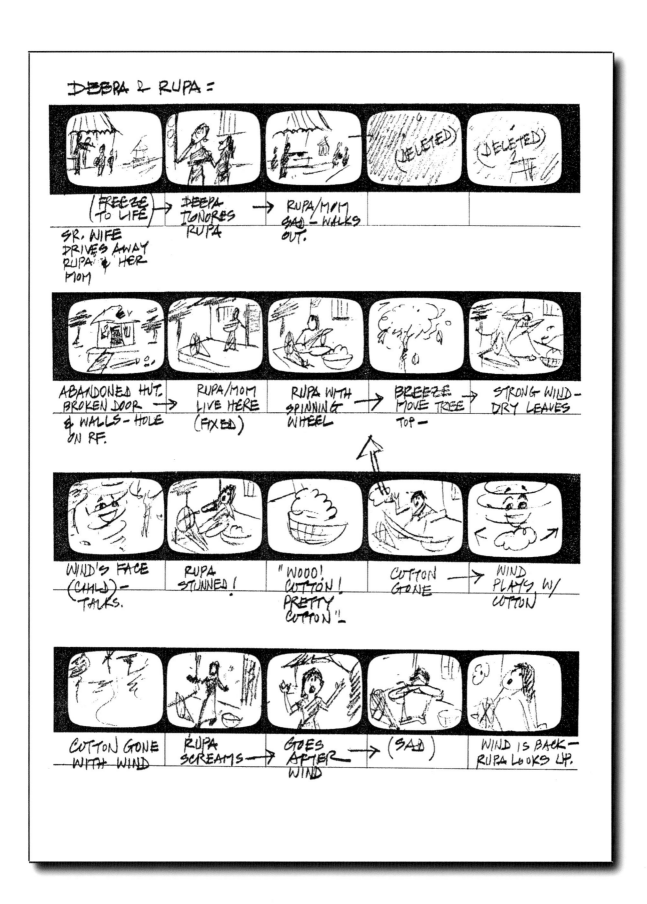

A page from the original quick-storyboard of *Deepa & Rupa: A Fairy Tale From India.*

Cut to SC 54
(same as SC 49)   SFX: water splash

(MS: Well, Rupa, Horse) / Prop: bucket with rope

(Rupa picks up the bucket and begins lowering it
into the well and talks)

Rupa: You have to bring the water up with the
       bucket, like this!

Horse: Oh! I didn t know that !!

Cut to SC 55
(same as SC 53)   SFX: water drip

(CU: Rupa) / Prop: bucket with rope

(She pulls the rope up and places the bucket on
the well rim as she talks)

Horse (OC): I am glad you stopped for me. Where
            are you going?

Rupa: To the moon. The old woman there has
            my cotton. But I don t even know if
            I can get there!

Horse (OC): You can if you ride a cloud. They fly
            up to the moon all the time, you know.
            Just go on to the East - that way!

(Rupa turns to look to the East)

While a quick-storyboard was designed to hold the story together, a detailed storyboard gave the specifics of camera treatment, action, prop details and sound effects. Sorcar always believed in having a thoroughly detailed storyboard which helps in having a quality production. Note how the black and white handsketch of scene 54 above is transformed into the colored animation below. The storyboard was used for all animation, live action and combination of the two in the studio.

(top) Detailed storyboard of scenes 54 and 55.
(bottom) Color animation of scene 54.

Handpainted Scenes

Just before the computer revolution, Sorcar painted all background scenes by hand on newsprint—a form that he prefers to use even today.

Watercolor traditionally had the problem of warping the paper. So during the camera shots, they needed to be placed under a sheet of glass. This reduced the brightness and lowered the picture quality. In order to increase brightness, supplementary task lights were added. But this gave rise to new problems as their reflections were visible.

Sorcar avoided traditional techniques and came up with the original idea of painting on newsprint with oil-based markers—which solved the problem. This saved time and money without compromising quality.

The background scenes were so impressive, they were even exhibited in art galleries as works of classic art.

(top left) Haystack.
(top right) Under the Banyan tree.
(bottom) Interior of Rupa's home.

"Looks like P.C. Sorcar's son wields the same magic that his father did—only in a different sphere."

The Illustrated Weekly of India
Weekend Edition
India
December 22-23, 1990

Unable to get any funding, Sorcar financed *Deepa & Rupa* himself. He used family members and friends for the cast. His daughter, Piya, played Rupa, and his wife, Shikha, played Rupa's mother, while designing costumes for the film. Piya received a nomination for the Heartland Regional Emmy Award for Outstanding Acting, and the animation went on to receive a host of international awards including the Golden Plaque at the Chicago International Film Festival.

(top left) A trail in the forest.
(top right) Sharmishtha Arora as the Moon Lady.
(bottom left) Mr. Horse awaits Rupa's arrival from the cloud.
(bottom right) Rupa talks to the old Banyan tree.

"Not only was it an important fairy tale for young children, but also had educational values for high-school students studying the many uses of computers."

Carolyn R. Jones
Multi-Cultural Educational Coordinator
Aurora Public Schools
Colorado, USA

The Challenge of Weaving Animation with Live Action

Since computers were still a new product, Sorcar had to hand-draw the movements of the characters frame-by-frame. Afterwards, each image was captured by a video camera and imported on to the computer. Towards the end of the 80's, he started using computers to help generate the "in-betweens" between the "extremes" of the movements that were still hand-drawn.

Sorcar then used the chroma-key technology with a blue room at a local professional studio to shoot the live action along with the animation to mix the two.

Directing the live actor to act with an animated character was always a challenge, as the acting was done with an imaginary character. Proper eye contact, body movement, flow of conversational reactions and correct lighting were the critical challenges to produce a convincing mix.

Deepa and Rupa had both technical sophistication and the warmth of a family production. It felt real and live, like grandma's tale.

(top left) A scene of Rupa, played by Piya Sorcar, interacting with an animated cow in *Deepa & Rupa*.
(top right) Sunita Budhiraja, on left, as Deepa's mother. Deepa played by Deepa Reddy.
(bottom) Rupa gives the animated character a hug.

Daily Camera

8A DAILY CAMERA   Thursday, September 13, 1990

ENTERTAINMENT

Engineer creates TV fable on computer

Video by Denverite airs tonight, Sunday

By RONDA HASKINS
Camera Television Editor

This is the story of a girl whose father sends her on a magical journey to the moon — in his spare time from his job as a Denver electrical engineer.

Or electrical whiz, to be more precise. Manick Sorcar, 44, is currently at work designing the lighting for the concourses and underground railway for Denver's new international airport. He's the author of three lighting-design books — one used by the University of Colorado.

But Sorcar doesn't just figure out where the light bulbs go. He's interested in lighting of different sort — the ill... mination offe... "Deepa & R... Fro... Ch...

pleasant music — he did similar work in India for his father, who was a professional magician.

With animating software, videotape and a personal computer, Sorcar spent about three years making his fairy tale, keeping production costs low. "I'm no Walt Disney," he says modestly. But comparing Sorcar's results with tape and computer to those more traditional animations seen on Saturday mornings, he just about could be Hanna-Barbera.

But competing with co... cial cartoons... intent;... glimp... cul...

"*Deepa & Rupa* is a charming little story that would be right at home in the PBS '*Long Ago and Far Away*' story telling anthology, in quality of content as well as production... Comparing Sorcar's results with tape and computer to those more traditional animation seen on Saturday mornings, he just about could be Hanna-Barbera."

Ronda Haskins
The Daily Camera
USA
September 13, 1990

AN ANANDABAZAR PUBLICATION □ VOL 3 □ ISSUE 6

প্রবাসী আনন্দবাজার

মার্কিন মুলুকে বাংলার রূপকথা

(top) Newspaper clipping from *The Daily Camera* that gave rave reviews on *Deepa & Rupa* after it premiered on television.
(bottom) The success story of *Deepa & Rupa* was breaking news in *Prabasi Anandabazar,* the international edition of the popular Indian newspaper.

Rocky Mountain News   Sat., April 27, 1991

ENTERTAINMENT WATCH

From left, Manick Sorcar and daughter Piya with Gerald Goldberg, president of the International Film and TV Festival of New York.

A fairy tale ending for Golden producer

Golden producer Manick Sorcar's *Deepa & Rupa: A Fairytale from India* recieved The Golden Plaque at the 26th Annual Chicago International Film and Television Festival in the Children's Television Program category. The video has also won a silver and a bronze medal at the 33rd Annual International Film and TV Festival of New York. In head-to-head competition, it topped the Children's Workshop's *Sesame Street* and Hanna-Barbera's *The Greatest Adventure* at the latter event. The animated tele-movie, which premiered on public television in Denver last year, is intended as a cultural bridge between East and West.

"Manick Sorcar has created a masterpiece with the live action—animation movie *Deepa & Rupa*... The son of legendary figure continues to spread stardust in a hi-tech manner."

The Link
Vancouver, B.C., Canada
August 8, 1992

★★★★   3:279

Deepa and Rupa: A Fairy Tale from India

Live action, Animation. Manick Sorcar Productions. Copyright 1990. Available from Barr Films. 30 min. Color. $295, public perf.

ISBN 1-56092-495-0
398.2 Children's films | |
Fairy tales—India | | Animated films

AUDIENCE: Primary to Intermediate

This video is aimed at children in the primary and intermediate grades. It recounts an Indian fairy tale of honesty and greed by skillfully interweaving animation with live-action characters. The opening shots show a book, and as the pages turn, the characters come alive against a background of colorful, if static, animation.

Deepa and Rupa are stepsisters who live in the state of Bengal, India. They have different mothers, but the same father (he has two wives at the same time). After their father's death, the senior wife, Deepa's mother, throws the junior wife and her daughter Rupa out of the house. They have to find an old hut to live in and weave cotton into thread to pay for food. One day, the Laughing Wind steals Rupa's cotton and she journeys to his grandmother, the Old Woman in the Moon, to get it back. Along the way, Rupa helps a talking cow and a horse. Because of her kindness, the old woman bestows riches on her. Deepa discovers Rupa's riches and follows the same path, but she does not help others, cheats the old woman, and ends up with nothing.

Technically, the combination of live actresses and animated, anthropomorphic characters works well. The two different techniques blend well together and look natural, and the acting is good (although Deepa sounds like a typical American teenager of the 1990s). The music, consisting of sitar, tabla, and synthesizer, reflects the action. The off-screen narrator speaks clearly. The action is well paced and easy to follow.

The morals presented in this story will not go out of date and the video captures the flavor and fantasy of another culture. This video may be best suited to school libraries as an introduction to different cultures and their folklore and for public libraries that can afford the public performance price.

—*Sharon G. Almquist*

Sharon G. Almquist
Video Rating Guide for Libraries
USA
Volume 3, Number 1

(left) Newspaper clipping from *The Rocky Mountain News* that describes Sorcar's success with *Deepa & Rupa*, surpassing *Sesame Street* and Hanna-Barbera's *The Greatest Adventure* at the International Film Festival of New York.

(right) A four-star ("excellent") rating for *Deepa & Rupa* by the *Video Rating Guide for Libraries* publication. The video distributor had sold each video cassette for $295. Sorcar took over the distribution to make it easily affordable for children, selling the videos at $10 each.

Awards & Accolades

GOLD PLAQUE in Children's Television Programming, 26th Chicago International Film & TV Festival, Chicago

SILVER PLAQUE in Animation 26th Chicago International Film & TV Festival, Chicago

GOLDEN EAGLE in Overall Achievement Council on International Non-Theatrical Events (CINE), Washington D.C.

SILVER MEDAL in Animation 33rd International Film & TV Festival of New York, New York

BRONZE MEDAL in Children's Programming 33rd International Film & TV Festival of New York, New York

BRONZE PLAQUE in Animation Association of Visual Communicators, California

CINDY AWARD in Art Direction Association of Visual Communicators, California

HONORABLE MENTION in Children's Education 38th Columbus International Film & Video Festival, Ohio

NOMINATIONS FOR HEARTLAND REGIONAL EMMY AWARDS for Outstanding Youth/Children's Programming, Outstanding Individual Craft—Animation, and Outstanding Individual Craft—Acting/Performing.

(top) Some of Manick Sorcar's accolades.

- *Deepa & Rupa: A Fairy Tale From India* was recorded as India's first animation mixed with live action.

- *Deepa & Rupa* won in a head-to-head competition with the Children's Workshop's *Sesame Street* and Hanna-Barbera's *The Greatest Adventure*, as well as 3,000 entries from 29 countries.

THE COLORADO CHAPTER OF
THE NATIONAL ACADEMY OF TELEVISION ARTS AND SCIENCES

1990-1991 HEARTLAND REGIONAL EMMY AWARDS
Honors
MANICK SORCAR
"DEEPA & RUPA: A FAIRYTALE FROM INDIA"
MANICK SORCAR PRODUCTIONS
Nominated For
OUTSTANDING INDIVIDUAL CRAFT: ANIMATION

President

(top) Manick & Piya Sorcar with Gerald Goldberg, President of the International Film & TV Festival of New York, after receiving their medals at the award ceremony.
(inset) Heartland Regional Emmy award nomination for Sorcar's "Outstanding Individual Craft: Animation."

The Sage & the Mouse

Sorcar's next production was a predominantly computer-drawn animation. It was based on one of the tales from *The Panchatantra*, which means, "five ways that helps human beings succeed in life." According to Indian tradition, they were written around 200 B.C. by Pandit Vishnu Sharma, a sage who was invited by the king to teach his sons the ways of the world. Vishnu Sharma gave the teachings through a series of animal fables and each one had a moral.

Sorcar chose the story of *The Sage & the Mouse*, which taught humility as a virtue. *The Sage & the Mouse* received a host of awards and international recognition.

(top) An image from *The Sage & The Mouse*.

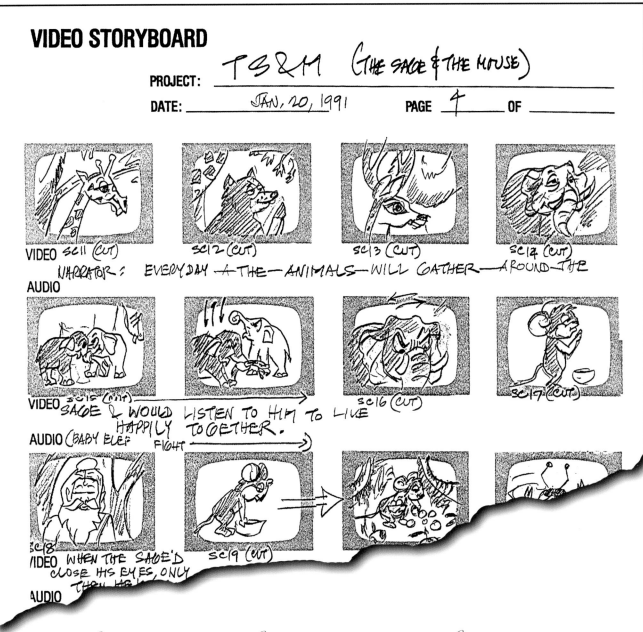

VIDEO SC11 (CUT)   SC12 (CUT)   SC13 (CUT)   SC14 (CUT)

AUDIO   NARRATOR: EVERYDAY THE ANIMALS WILL GATHER AROUND THE

VIDEO SC15 (CUT)   SC16 (CUT)   SC17 (CUT)

AUDIO (BABY ELEF FIGHT   ) SAGE & WOULD LISTEN TO HIM TO LIVE HAPPILY TOGETHER.

SC18

VIDEO   WHEN THE SAGE'D CLOSE HIS EYES, ONLY   SC19 (CUT)

AUDIO

Does the Computer Solve Animation Problems?

There is a general concept that the computer solves all problems of manual labor associated with animation. This is far from the truth, explains Sorcar:

"Computer or not, animation still involves a laborious process including story selection, screenplay development, building a storyboard, sound track recording, animating and editing. While the computer helps in many things, animation is still fundamentally dependent on the skill of the animator. For a quality animation, the animator draws the key action (extreme points) by hand with the help of his imagination. The 'in-between' frames are either generated by computer or by hand."

For both *The Sage & the Mouse* and *Sniff*, Sorcar experimented and used the computer to paint almost all of the background scenes. For animated movements, he drew them by hand following the storyboard. These actions were then used as a guide to be developed by the computer, and generate the "in-betweens." For critical scenes where actions needed to be warm and natural, he hand-sketched each and every frame and then captured them with a camera on the computer.

(top) A part of the original quick-storyboard of *The Sage & The Mouse*.

The 11-minute animation used 14,400 frames all developed by Sorcar on his personal computer.

(top) The sage and his disciples in the forest.
(bottom) A scene from *The Sage & The Mouse*.

Awards & Accolades

GOLD MEDAL in Original Music
36th International Film & TV Festival of New York, New York

SILVER MEDAL in Children's Programming
36th International Film & TV Festival of New York, New York

BRONZE PLAQUE in Animation
41st Columbus International Film & Video Festival, Ohio

(top) Sorcar receives the Gold Medal at the 36th International Film & TV Festival of New York, USA.
(bottom) Sorcar receives the Bronze Plaque at the 41st Columbus International Film & Video Festival in Ohio, USA.

Sniff (Gandhabichar)

Along with *The Sage & the Mouse*, Sorcar produced another animation film titled *Sniff* in 1993. *Sniff* was based on the works of the illustrious Bengali poet and playwright, Sukumar Ray, who has been often compared to Lewis Carroll. Ray is best known for his collection of poems, *Abol Tabol*, meaning, "literary nonsense." His works were also a satirical comment on life during the British Raj, which Sorcar portrayed with brilliant humor! *Sniff* is a laugh-out-loud animation with unforgettable characters that adults and kids can fall in love with. The animation has technical sophistication as well as a rich Indian flavor. Both the films premiered on the Denver PBS channel on July 1, 1993 and aired again on July 4, the American Independence Day.

(top) A scene from *Sniff*.

Scenes From Sniff and Its Famous Characters

(top) Raja (the King).
(bottom left) Kotal (the Soldier-in-Chief).
(bottom right) Nazir (the old man).

Awards & Accolades

GOLDEN EAGLE *in Overall Achievement*
Council on International Non-Theatrical Events (CINE),
Washington D.C.

FINALIST *in Children's Programming*
36th International Film & TV Festival of New York, New York

• *Sniff* (Gandhabichar) was recorded as the first animation based on Sukumar Ray's *Abol Tabol.*

• *Sniff* is a product of over 23,421 frames.

"Manick Sorcar brings to life the unforgettable characters of 'Gandhabichar.' "

The Statesman,
Kolkata, India

"So far, he has been nothing but successful. In the last decade Manick has major contributions to children's arts and cultural education through a series of self-developed animated programs."

The Denver Post
Colorado Living section
USA
July 1, 1993

(top) Sorcar with the Council on International Non-Theatrical Events (C.I.N.E.) Golden Eagle, celebrating with the cast of *Sniff.* From top left going clockwise, Nazir, Manick, the King, Ram Narayan Patra, and Bheem Singh.

The Woodcutter's Daughter

Manick Sorcar's next major production was another half-hour animation weaved with live action. *The Woodcutter's Daughter*, which recreates another tale from *The Panchatantra*, the classic book of moral fables of India, premiered on Rocky Mountain PBS (KRMA-TV) in Denver, Colorado, USA on September 7, 1997. It received rave reviews and great responses from schools, and was a Finalist in the Children's Program category at the 40th Annual International Film Festival of New York.

Sorcar's animation series became so popular that they were repeatedly shown on the mid-western PBS television stations. In 2008, it ran for the sixteenth consecutive year.

(top) Payal Sorcar interacting with her friend, an animated squirrel in *The Woodcutter's Daughter*.

Awards & Accolades

FINALIST *in Children's Programming*
40th International Film & TV Festival of New York, New York

(top) A scene from *The Woodcutter's Daughter*. From left, Shubha Mehra, Payal Sorcar, and Abhay Kale.
(bottom) A scene from *The Woodcutter's Daughter*.

The Denver Post / Dave Buresh

Manick Sorcar is an engineer by day, but at night he becomes a one-man animation company, working magic in his basement studio.

Animation man

Sorcar's videos build 'cultural bridge'

By Diane Eicher
Denver Post Staff Writer

By day, Manick Sorcar is an engineer who specializes in lighting design — staid, formal work that relies on a knowledge of science and technical skill.

He's done projects for the palaces of Saudi Arabian princes and designed the lighting for the concourses at Denver International Airport.

He's written three textbooks on the subject.

But by night — and frequently well into the early hours before dawn — Sorcar undergoes what he calls a "sort of Dr. Jekyll-Mr. Hyde" transformation: He becomes an artist, where the rules of engineering no longer apply.

Versatile artist

He has excelled in a variety of media, like watercolors and acrylics, and also in some very non-traditional, almost odd outlets, like sculpture out of Styrofoam, painting with seeds, and tiny ink portraits of famous people on peanuts (Jimmy Carter) and grains of rice (Abraham Lincoln).

He draws cartoons that are run in some international papers, and had a show last year at Foothills Art Center that showcased his unique portraits of personalities constructed entirely of newspaper clippings.

But there's another kind of art that's been keeping him up well

Payal Sorcar, 16, talks to an antimated squirrel in her father's fourth animated video, 'The Woodcutter's Daughter.'

From left, Shubha Mehra, Payal Sorcar and Abhay Kale in 'The Woodcutter's Daughter.'

ON TV

WHAT: Premiere of Manick Sorcar's animated/live action video, 'The Woodcutter's Daughter,' based on a folktale from India
WHEN: 9 a.m. Sunday, on KRMA-Channel 6

into the night: Sorcar is also a one-man animation company, producing children's videos in his basement on a bank of computer screens.

The videos are based on folktales from his native India — stories he recalls his grandmother telling him, each with a moral just as apt for today's world as when the narratives were handed down centuries ago.

And now his fourth video, "The Woodcutter's Daughter," will premiere at 9 a.m. Sunday on KRMA-Channel 6, the local affiliate.

It's produced in [...] animation [...] tion.

The [...] 16-ye[...] olde[...] w[...]

hopes will help the children of both nations better understand the other.

The videos got their start more than a decade ago when Sorcar saw his daughters, then 8 and 5, forsaking the family's Indian ways for the American lifestyle they were picking up in schools in Jefferson County, where the family has lived for 20 years.

Sorcar's mother came for a visit from India, and the children spoke English to her — which appalled grandma. Sorcar and his wife, Shikha, were concerned, too: "We didn't want them to forget our culture," he said.

Since the couple's arri[...] U.S. in 1970, they h[...] embrace both [...] their Indian [...] thorou[...] ways [...] cou[...]

"Manick Sorcar is an engineer by day, but at night he becomes a one-man animation company, working magic in his basement studio."

The Denver Post
USA
September 4, 1997

(top) Front page of the article on Sorcar in *The Denver Post.*

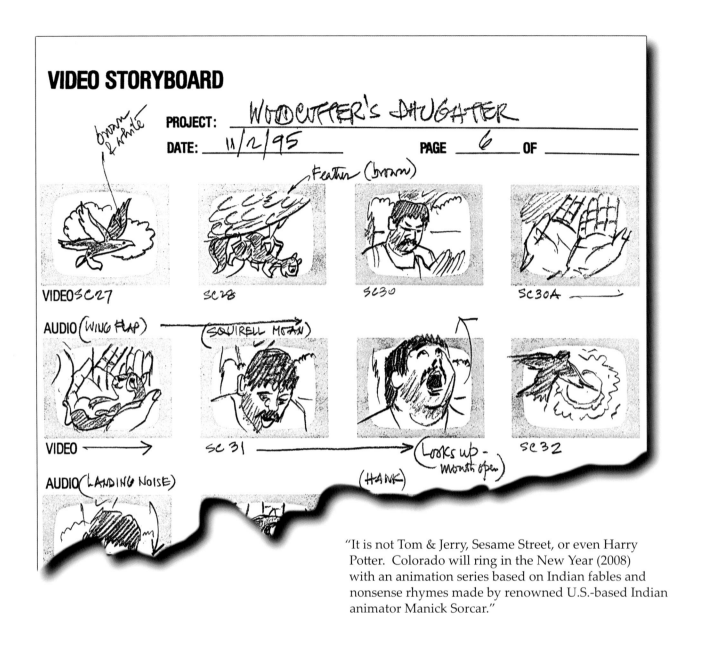

VIDEO STORYBOARD

PROJECT: WOODCUTTER'S DAUGHTER

DATE: 11/2/95   PAGE 6 OF _____

brown & white

Feather (brown)

VIDEO SC27   SC28   SC30   SC30A

AUDIO (WING FLAP)   (SQUIRELL MOAN)

VIDEO →   SC31   (Looks up - mouth open)   SC32

AUDIO (LANDING NOISE)   (HAWK)

"It is not Tom & Jerry, Sesame Street, or even Harry Potter. Colorado will ring in the New Year (2008) with an animation series based on Indian fables and nonsense rhymes made by renowned U.S.-based Indian animator Manick Sorcar."

Sify News
Internet publication

In a letter to Manick Sorcar from Prof. Mishra while visiting family in the USA:

"Let me first heartily congratulate you. I have seen this morning on the television, 'The Woodcutter's Daughter,' based on the everlasting Indian Tale of the 'Panchatantra,' which was very well directed and superbly produced by you. All the participants in this animated video deserve congratulations, too... I see in you a true Indian in the American pot. You are really a worthy son of a worthy father."

Prof. Dr. Jayamanta Mishra, M.A., Ph.D
Recipient of President's Award
Ex-Vice Chancellor of K.S.D.S. University, Darbhanga, India
September 7, 1997

(top) Part of the storyboard for *The Woodcutter's Daughter.*

The Rule of Twenty-One

The success with *Sniff* based on Ray's *Gandhabichar* was a great source of inspiration to debut Sorcar's second Bengali animation, *The Rule of Twenty-One*. It was adapted from Sukumar Ray's famous non-sense poem, *Ekushe Aine*.

(top) Image from *Rule of Twenty-One*.
(bottom) The Poet of *Rule of Twenty-One*.

(top) Kaji (the judge), with Peyada (the policeman).
(bottom left) The land of funny rules: slipping and falling is strictly prohibited.
(bottom right) Peoples' teeth were regularly inspected by the police. Having a loose tooth is subject to penalty.

"I was much impressed by how you have built a story out of a nonsense poem, and developed the plots so meticulously—each climaxing to a great comedy."

Lance Carwile
Chairman, Entertainment Division
Columbus International Film &
Video Festival
USA

Awards & Accolades

BRONZE PLAQUE *in Animation*
51st Columbus International Film & Video Festival, Ohio

(top) Sorcar receives the Bronze Plaque from Lance Carwile, Chairman of the Entertainment Division, at the 51st Columbus International Film & Video Festival.
(bottom) Sorcar is shown being interviewed by NTD-TV, based in Taipei, Taiwan and New York, USA, after receiving the award.

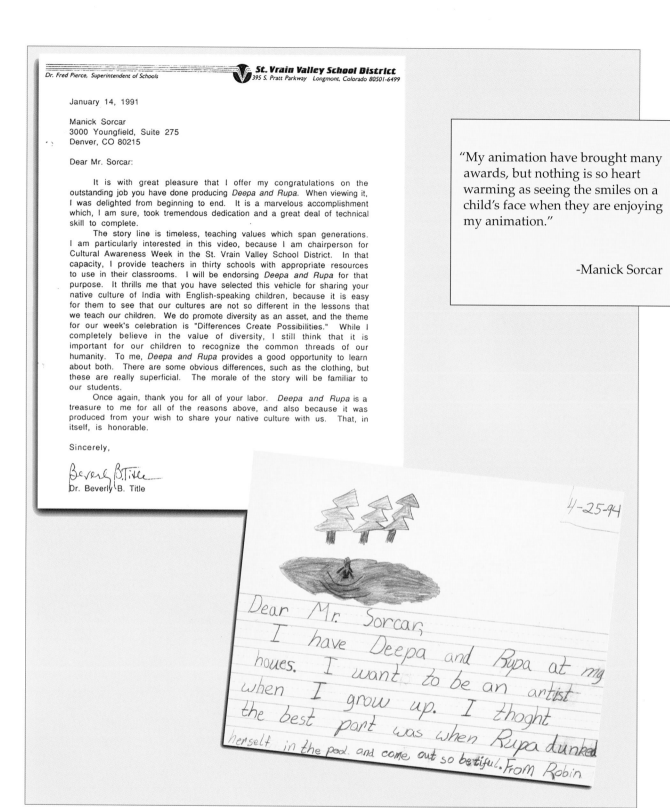

St. Vrain Valley School District
Dr. Fred Pierce, Superintendent of Schools
395 S. Pratt Parkway Longmont, Colorado 80501-6499

January 14, 1991

Manick Sorcar
3000 Youngfield, Suite 275
Denver, CO 80215

Dear Mr. Sorcar:

It is with great pleasure that I offer my congratulations on the outstanding job you have done producing *Deepa and Rupa*. When viewing it, I was delighted from beginning to end. It is a marvelous accomplishment which, I am sure, took tremendous dedication and a great deal of technical skill to complete.

The story line is timeless, teaching values which span generations. I am particularly interested in this video, because I am chairperson for Cultural Awareness Week in the St. Vrain Valley School District. In that capacity, I provide teachers in thirty schools with appropriate resources to use in their classrooms. I will be endorsing *Deepa and Rupa* for that purpose. It thrills me that you have selected this vehicle for sharing your native culture of India with English-speaking children, because it is easy for them to see that our cultures are not so different in the lessons that we teach our children. We do promote diversity as an asset, and the theme for our week's celebration is "Differences Create Possibilities." While I completely believe in the value of diversity, I still think that it is important for our children to recognize the common threads of our humanity. To me, *Deepa and Rupa* provides a good opportunity to learn about both. There are some obvious differences, such as the clothing, but these are really superficial. The morale of the story will be familiar to our students.

Once again, thank you for all of your labor. *Deepa and Rupa* is a treasure to me for all of the reasons above, and also because it was produced from your wish to share your native culture with us. That, in itself, is honorable.

Sincerely,

Dr. Beverly B. Title

"My animation have brought many awards, but nothing is so heart warming as seeing the smiles on a child's face when they are enjoying my animation."

-Manick Sorcar

4-25-94

Dear Mr. Sorcar,
I have Deepa and Rupa at my houes. I want to be an artist when I grow up. I thoght the best part was when Rupa dunked herself in the pool and come out so betiful. From Robin

Cultural Bridge at Grass-Root Level

The success of Sorcar's animation films were soon stapled to the U.S. elementary schools—where he was frequently invited to make presentations of the animation films, and provide a workshop or Q/A session with the children.

(top) Letter from Dr. Beverly B. Title from the St. Vrain Valley School District in Colorado, USA praising Sorcar for his work in spreading cultural education through his animation.
(bottom) Letter from a student at Niwot Elementary sharing her favorite scene in *Deepa & Rupa*.

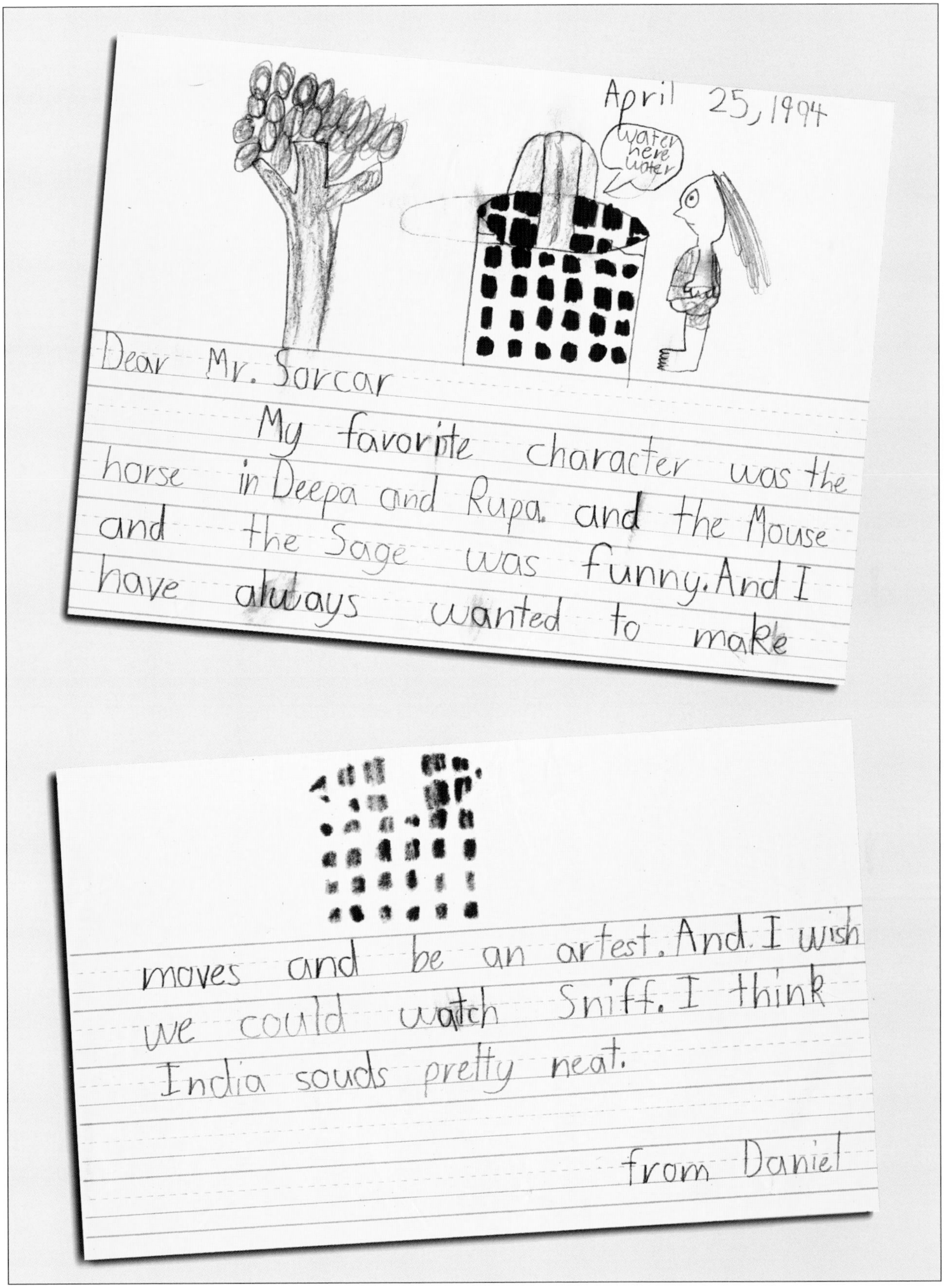

April 25, 1994

Dear Mr. Sorcar

My favorite character was the horse in Deepa and Rupa. and the Mouse and the Sage was funny. And I have always wanted to make

moves and be an artest. And I wish we could watch Sniff. I think India souds pretty neat.

from Daniel

(top) Another letter from a student of Niwot Elementary after he saw Sorcar's animation presentation, who thought India sounded "pretty neat!"

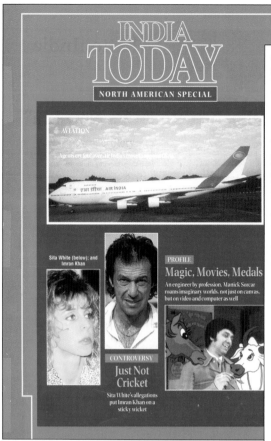

"He doesn't exactly pull rabbits out of a hat, but his sleight of hand is worthy of a magician... What started out as efforts to introduce his daughters to their heritage has evolved into award-winning films."

Lavina Melwani
India Today
February 15, 1997

Manick Sorcar—One of The Top 100 People

"An award-winning artist in multimedia, an internationally published cartoonist, a musician and a magician, Manick Sorcar spends his days as president and chief electrical engineer of Butterweck-Sorcar Engineering in Denver. During the nights, Sorcar follows his artistic side."

Jefferson The Magazine
Winter '97-'98 Issue
USA
p. 77

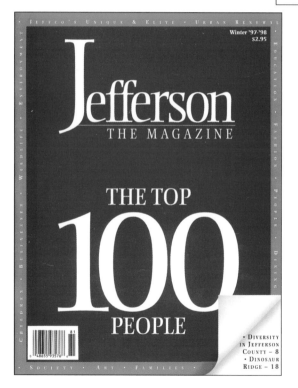

(top) Sorcar on the cover of *India Today,* the respected magazine of India, and the article on his work in the North American Special, February 15, 1997.

(bottom left) Cover of *Jefferson The Magazine*, USA, Winter '97-'98 Issue.

(bottom right) Manick Sorcar selected as one of the "Top 100 People" in Artworld, page 77.

Sorcar was invited to hold a workshop at the 4th Annual Midwestern Indian-American Student Conference (MIASC) at the University of Michigan in Ann Arbor, Michigan, USA where the mission statement was *2000 Reflections: Discovering Your Inspirational Light*. The conference was attended by students from 20 universities across the nation. In his topic, "Indian Culture: Will Our Children Know?" Sorcar set an example of how one can stay connected with one's roots in a melting pot of cultures. The audience loved his presentation and animation films, and due to heavy demand, it was presented three times.

"Sorcar reminded participants how difficult it can be to preserve rich, traditional heritage in the vastly different contemporary American culture."

The Michigan Daily
USA
January 24, 2000

Cultural Bridge at an Academic Level

In 2005, Wendy Jensen, a fine arts major at the Savannah College of Art and Design in Savannah, Georgia, USA, wrote a thesis paper titled, "Manick Sorcar Animation That Teaches Indian Culture." Jensen's dissertation evaluates Sorcar's achievements in spreading cultural diversity through animation.

India Abroad August 12, 2005   **Community**News   C5

Sorcar's cartoons animate American student

SUMAN GUHA MOZUMDER

Like many other American children, **Wendy M Jensen**, 22 of New Jersey grew up watching Disney cartoons on television, but by the time she went to college to major in 3D animation, she had stopped raving about it.

"I realized I was not a big fan of the likes of Disney and the kind of things they create because I felt they are too commercial," said the student of Savannah College of Art and Design.

So, when Jensen, who has a bachelor in fine arts with a double major in animation and visual effects, had to do her dissertation in May this year as part of her course study, she chose to write not about American animation filmmakers of the likes of Disney, but about **Manick Sorcar**, an award-winning animation filmmaker from India, and brother of magician **P C Sorcar**.

"His creations are unique in the sense that he never wanted to compete with commercial car-

toons, but tried to show American children that other cultures and countries have well-known fables that fit with the American culture," Jensen told *India Abroad*. "I was really inspired by the fact that he did not do whatever he did for money or fame or glory but because he enjoyed what he was doing."

Sorcar, who runs an engineering firm based in Denver, Colorado, has produced several children's favorites animations, based on Indian fables, like *Deepa and Rupa*, the *Sage and Mouse* and the *Rule of Twenty-one*.

Jensen's research paper *Manick Sorcar: Animations that Teach Indian Cultures*, analyzes Sorcar's work and its impact. Jensen said she wants to show first hand things that he knows about India to the kids of America, she said, quoting from *Denver Post* to which Sorcar gave an interview. 'My work is not only entertainment but serves as a cultural bridge between India and the

■ Wendy Jensen (left), and Manick Sorcar with some of his toon characters (right)

United States,' he had said then.

That is what Jensen liked most about Sorcar.

Though the two had never met and communicated solely though e-mails, Jensen said his style impressed her before she chose to write her dissertation on Sorcar.

"I was inspired by the fact that he did not do what he did because of money or fame or glory but (*he did what he did*) because he enjoyed what he did," she said. "It was interesting to see his person-

al style come out."

For example, she said, *Deepa and Rupa* started off pretty hard up, but "then that is what life is all about.

"Disney makes it all cute and nice, but Sorcar showed truly that there could be greedy and selfish people on earth," Jensen said, adding, "one could see the difference."

In her research paper, she wrote that Sorcar's work mainly reaches out to the younger audi-

ence that mixes eastern with western ideas to help bridge cultural differences.

She noted that working out of his basement he is able to separate himself from the sciences and put himself into a world of artistic inspiration.

'Sorcar does a wonderful job of combining the cultures to make it easy and fun for us to learn about the diversity as well as the similarities in our cultures. These two can create a wonderful outcome of knowledge that everyone can learn from,' Jensen wrote in the paper.

One thing about Sorcar that attracted Jensen to do her dissertation on him is Sorcar's ability to strike a balance between two cultures.

"During my e-mail exchanges, I was impressed by the fact that he was able to keep his culture. When he moved here, he could have easily integrated to our culture and society and could have ditched his culture," Jensen said. "But he did not."

"His creations are unique in the sense that he never wanted to compete with commercial cartoons, but tried to show American children that other cultures and countries have well-known fables that fit with the American culture."

Wendy Jensen, *India Abroad* interview
Community News Section
August 12, 2005

(top) University of Michigan in Ann Arbor, Michigan, USA.
(bottom) Article in *India Abroad* discussing Wendy Jensen's dissertation on Manick Sorcar's animation.

Film Festivals

(*top left*) Sorcar with his family and Ron Henderson, Executive Director of the 1998 Denver International Film Festival. *Deepa & Rupa, The Sage & The Mouse,* and *The Woodcutter's Daughter* were screened at the film festival, achieving recognition as the "Recommended Film of the Day." Prior to the show, Sorcar was formally introduced as "Director in Person" to the audience by Henderson.

(*top right*) Manick and Shikha with then Denver Mayor, Wellington Webb at the Denver International Film Festival.

(*bottom left*) Cover page of the 4th Annual Aurora Asian Film Festival brochure.

(*bottom right*) Interviewed by Brit Withey, the Program Director of the Denver Film Society, and Nancy Philips, the News Producer of the City of Aurora of KACT-TV, Channel 8 at the Aurora Asian Film Festival in 2001.

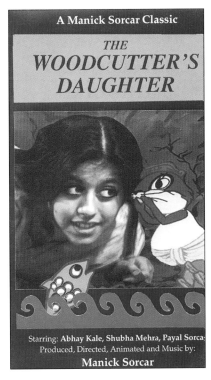

Sorcar's Animation Products

Images of the various animation videos, DVDs and music CDs of Manick Sorcar. They are available at libraries, bookstores, on-line stores, and Sorcar's website: www.manicksorcar.com

Upcoming Project #1

 Background scenes from Manick Sorcar's upcoming project. All scenes were digitally painted on the computer. He still draws the conceptual lines on a piece of paper, then transfers it on to the computer for final touches.

(top & bottom) Scenes from his Upcoming Project #1.

Upcoming Project #2

In his latest animation creation, Sorcar has used seeds of all colors and textures. The project is a story told through the digital lens, where seeds depict every single detail in each frame—from clothing and contours, to backgrounds and landscapes.

(top) This particular scene depicts a hummingbird traveling from one flower to another, gathering nectar. Scenes are made with seeds, lentils and cinnamon sticks.

ACT FIVE:
Laserist

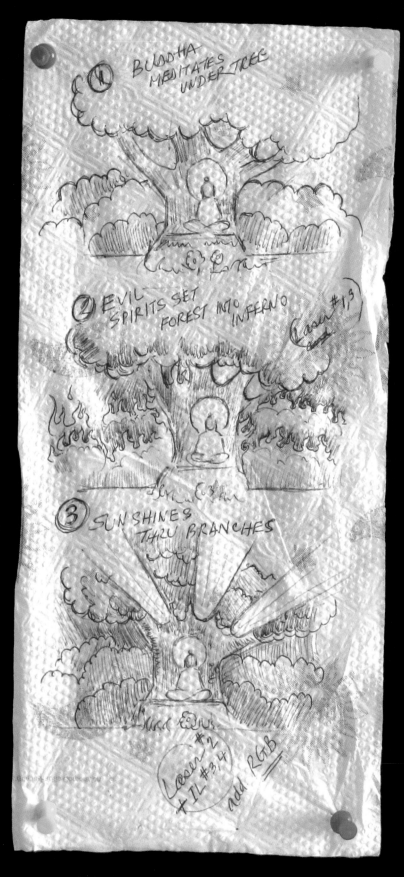

After the astonishing success of his animated films, one would think Sorcar had finally found his niche. However, he was still restless. He wanted to take his love for animation to an entirely new level, and combine it with his other interests in lighting, music, artistry and the performing arts. He was desperately seeking an opportunity to combine his engineering and artistic skills in one dynamic medium.

Then he found laser. Actually, he rediscovered laser.

For some time, he had been recommending laser to his clients as part of his consulting engineering service, for industrial and laboratory applications. One day, a thought struck him: Why not use laser for artistic animation? Says Sorcar, "that night I dreamed of the endless possibilities using laser. I was like a kid with a new favorite toy."

The ideas he had in mind had never been attempted before, and laser was notoriously difficult to work with. But soon, Sorcar was able to tame the strong, dangerous beam of light to act as a soft paintbrush. He started crafting laser art in both two and three dimensions, using space as the ultimate canvas. He saw infinite possibilities for using it on stage, and the dancing talents of his daughters was the basis of another new idea. Making a rather innovative leap, Sorcar combined live performers with life-size laser-animation on stage in a way the world had never seen before. Laser gave him the power to transport his audience to an imaginary world, and he decided to build a full-scale stage production around these techniques. He assembled a team of world-class performers, and started touring the world with elaborate productions like Synergy, Dancing with My Soul, Underwater Fantasy, Enlightenment of Buddha. The shows were an effervescent mix of laser, lighting, music, dance, and special effects that had captivated audience.

Incidentally, Sorcar's creative visions often came at unpredictable moments. For example, the idea of Enlightenment of Buddha struck him in the middle of a party. He immediately sketched out the scenes on a paper napkin, which later became a crucial part of the memorable show.

His amazing creations did not go unnoticed by the laser industry. On two separate occasions, Sorcar won first place and received the ILDA Artistic Award from the International Laser Display Association. The first award was for Enlightenment of Buddha, in Rimini, Italy, for Best Use of Laser on Stage. The second was for Reflection onboard the Carnival Imagination Caribbean cruise ship, for Best Laser Photography. This is the ultimate recognition for a laserist—equivalent to the Oscars for film actors.

Sorcar had invented a unique way to marry science and art, and had reached the pinnacle of success. It appears the magician has found his wand and is finally at peace with himself.

Or is he?

LaserLight Magic

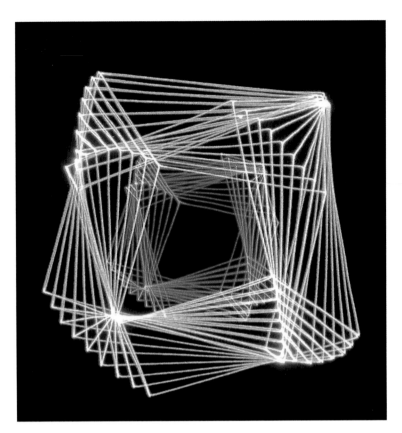

Laser Art

Laser is to Sorcar what a wand is to a magician. He uses it as a brush to paint a picture. The effects are so stunning that it is hard to imagine the complexity that lies beneath.

Explains Sorcar, "Laser art is not a standard computer graphic (like they are seen on a monitor or TV) or an image that is projected on a screen from a slide show. Laser art is actually a line drawing sketched on the computer as a series of electronic points which a single beam of laser follows to 'connect the dots' to give the optical illusion of a complete image on the screen. In reality, the single beam is stationary. With the help of the computer, two tiny mirrors are programmed to move the reflection of the beam very fast, precisely following the point-path. For a flat drawing it is projected on a screen. For mid-air 3-D patterns it is aimed in space above the audience. For animated movements, a series of drawings are drawn very much like in a traditional manner—by hand or with computers."

(left) Abstract laser art.
(right) Laser portrait of Gandhi.

Happy Nest

Laser art

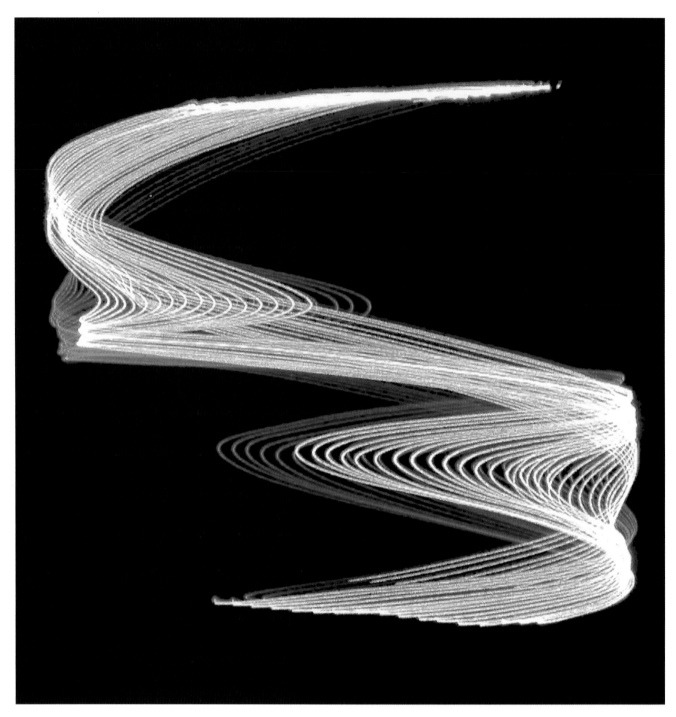

Dream

Laser art

Manick Sorcar: A Great American Success Story

"Manick Sorcar, a gifted electrical engineer based in Denver, Colorado, has come a long way from his profession to make a mark in the entertainment industry by skillfully blending science with art. And the effect has been electrifying."

Vasantha Arora
News India Times
USA
March 29, 2002

Pursuit

Laser art

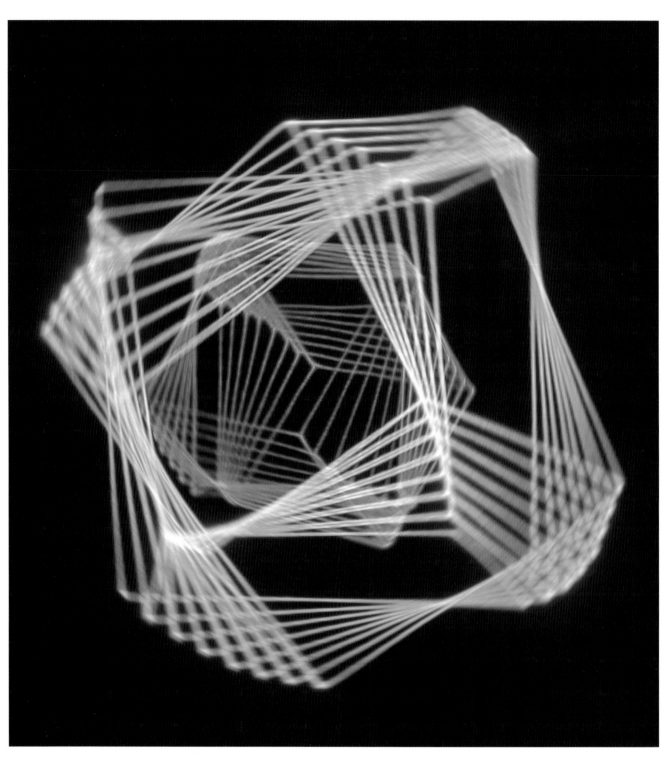

Psycho

Laser art

Silhouette

Laser art

Baby Ganesha

Laser art

Dreamcatcher

Laser art

Admiration

Laser art

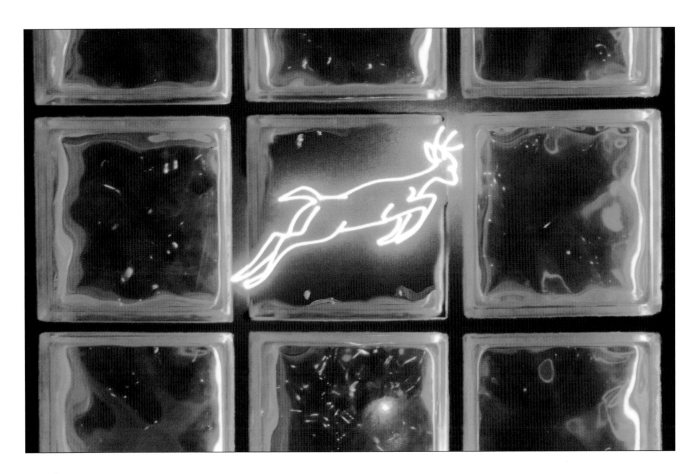

Escape

Laser art

A New Dawn

Laser art

The historical 2008 Presidential election had a significant impact on Sorcar. He made this laser art as a tribute to Barack Obama, the first African-American candidate to be nominated for the United States Presidency. It was created a day after Obama's nomination acceptance speech on August 28, 2008, at Invesco Field, Mile High Stadium in Denver, Colorado, USA. The laser image was projected on the wall adjacent to a window that let in the first rays of the morning sun.

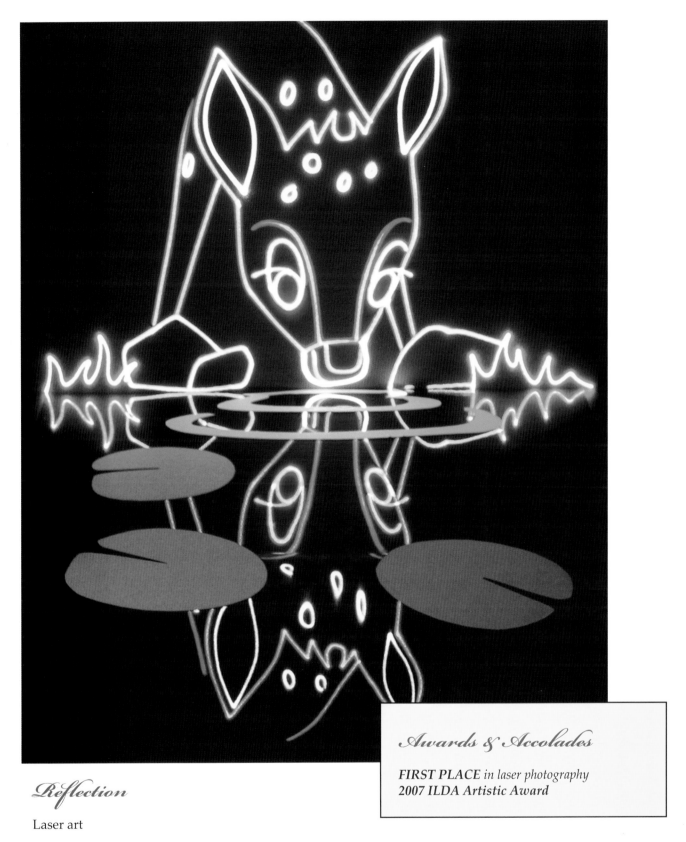

Reflection

Laser art

Awards & Accolades

FIRST PLACE *in laser photography*
2007 ILDA Artistic Award

On September 10, 2008, Sorcar's *Reflection* won the First Place for best laser photography and he was honored with the 2007 Artistic Award at the International Laser Display Association's (ILDA) annual conference. There were a total of 100 entries from 21 companies from all over the world. The international panel of judges unanimously selected *Reflection* as the winner, making Sorcar the first Asian to have received the Artistic Award twice. The ILDA Artistic Award is regarded as the Oscar of the laser industry. The trophy was handed to Sorcar onboard the Carnival Imagination during the ILDA Award Ceremony.

(top left)   Sorcar delivers his speech after receiving the ILDA Award trophy from Dirk Baur, Director of MediaLas Company of Germany.

(top right)   From left, clockwise: Tim Walsh, President of ILDA; Manick Sorcar of LaserLight Magic; Dirk Baur of MediaLas, Germany; and Alex Hennig of LOBO, Germany.

(bottom left)   Manick with Shikha at docking port of Nassau, Bahamas near Carnival Imagination.

(bottom right)   Manick and Shikha onboard Carnival Imagination.

"When doing a laser show without any live performance involved, I do not believe in confining it to just some beam shows married with popular music. I strongly believe that it is a medium through which we can bring people together for good causes and communicate with children in a visual language that they are attracted to."

Manick Sorcar
From *The Laserist* magazine article
USA
Summer 2008

The Laserist Interview: Manick Sorcar

"Manick Sorcar may be seen as an enigma, but it's much simpler just to call him 'Jekyll and Hyde.' The mediums he utilizes to produce art span far beyond lasers. Yet by day, he is a mild-mannered electrical engineer. *The Laserist* was fortunate enough to get Manick to speak with us about his formative years in the business, his dual careers, and the passion he brings to each moment on the planet."

From *The Laserist* magazine article
USA
Summer 2008

(top) Reflection was featured on the front cover of the International Laser Display Association's (ILDA) magazine, *The Laserist*, in their Summer 2008 issue. Inside, it ran a three-page interview of Sorcar.

"Manick Sorcar has painted Calcutta with the brushes of light…"

Ganashakti,
India
December 27, 1999

"Manick is an Extraordinary Talent… Today when we see American or British cartoons on TV they only entertain us for the period we watch them; we forget what we saw as soon as they are over. Each of Manick's animation leaves an impression—it keeps us thinking even long after it is over…"

Chandi Lahiri, Cartoonist
Songbad Ekhan Jemon
India
January, 2000

Laser Shows

Sorcar took laser art to another level by combining laser with animation. This resulted in a spectacular combination of 2-D and 3-D animated figures mixed with intelligent lighting. This time, space was his canvas.

Calcutta Forever: A Laser Fantasy

In the year 2000, on the occasion of Kolkata's (previously known as Calcutta) 300th anniversary, Sorcar was invited to do a special show at the World Bengali Conference. The venue was Nandan, the official theater of the Government of West Bengal. Sorcar's two-hour program consisted of his award-winning animation films, *Deepa & Rupa: A Fairy Tale From India, The Sage & The Mouse, Sniff,* and *The Woodcutter's Daughter.* The highlight of the evening was *Calcutta Forever: A Laser Fantasy,* an 8-minute laser documentary. With moving laser beams, Sorcar captured significant moments of Bengal's rich history spanning 300 years. The show was a smash hit, and the program was extended for an additional week.

(top) Howrah bridge in *Calcutta Forever. Calcutta Forever* was recorded as the first ever laser documentary to be shown in any theater.
(bottom) Manick and Shikha Sorcar in front of Nandan theater in Kolkata, India.

"Another Manick, another City of Joy. Sorcar's laser show *Calcutta Forever* is the first animation based on a theme to be screened at Nandan, which bags the honour of being the first Indian theater to do so."

The Telegraph
India
December 26, 1999

"The sheer virtuosity of the finished product is so impressive, that when watching the swift whirling of Sorcar's laser animation, the viewer forgets the painstaking months of computer programming, research, sketching, and technical organization that are behind Sorcar's magic."

The Statesman
India
December 23, 1999

(top left) Bidhan Chandra Roy, the second Chief Minister of West Bengal.
(top right) Raja Ram Mohan Roy, an important figure in the Bengal Renaissance.
(bottom left) Rabindra Nath Tagore, the legendary Bengali poet. He became Asia's first Nobel laureate when he won the 1913 Nobel Prize in Literature.
(bottom right) Sorcar is surrounded by his admirers while signing autographs.

A Touch of Water

   The Foothills Art Center's Grand Gala venue was transformed into an aquatic playground with Sorcar's laser show, *A Touch of Water*. It was held at the Colorado School of Mines in Golden, Colorado, USA in the year 2000.

(top) Image from the laser show, *A Touch of Water*.
(bottom) Sorcar with Bill Coors, Chairman of the world-famous Coors Brewing Company, who congratulated Sorcar for the "Outstanding laser-animation."

Biennial Convention

India Forever was the name of Sorcar's next production. Capturing over 4500 years of Indian history, it received a standing ovation at the National Federation of Indian-American Association's Biennial Convention held at East Brunswick, New Jersey, USA in the year 2000. Sorcar's achievements in art were also honored at the convention, as he was presented with the Excellence in Arts Award Plaque from U.S. Congressman Sam Gejdenson, Government of USA.

(top left) Image of a Harappa seal seen in *India Forever*.
(top right) Image of the Taj Mahal in *India Forever*.
(bottom right) Sorcar receiving the Excellence in Arts Plaque from Congressman Sam Gejdenson (D-CT, 2nd District).

International Center of the Broadmoor Hotel

At the Smith-Barney Citigroup Conference in 2004, Sorcar had presented a laser show for the event held at the International Center of the famous Broadmoor Hotel of Colorado Springs, Colorado, USA. In addition to projecting custom-animated figures running in tune with a live-concert group, the show contained a variety of overhead laser effects such as beams, fans, tunnels, waves, etc.

(top) A laser spectacle on display at the conference.
(bottom) A view of the crowd as they enjoy Sorcar's laser show on display with live performers on stage.

Celebrate Denver: A Smile-High Laser Show

Sorcar had the honor of being the lighting engineer of record for the Colorado Convention Center. He also added a sparkle to the Grand Opening Gala in 2004 with his laser show, *Celebrate Denver.* The show was such a crowd-puller, that the fire department had to intervene to avoid overcrowding. The 12-minute laser show captured the city's 146 year-old history presented through laser-animation and spectacular overhead visual effects, in combination with intelligent lighting and music. To meet the demand, it was shown once every hour, on the hour, starting from 6 p.m. to 11 p.m.

(top) Laser rays above the audience.
(bottom) Laser images of former Denver Mayor Wellington Webb (left), and current Mayor John Hickenlooper (right), as part of the laser show, *Celebrate Denver.*

(top) A captivated audience at Sorcar's show, *Celebrate Denver.* An overflow of people stood at the back and sat on the floor. The general comment was, "This is one show we cannot miss."
(bottom) Stage setting as seen prior to and after the show. By popular demand, there was a show on the hour, every hour, from 6 p.m. to 11 p.m.

Feel Like a Kid Again (Pepsi Center)

Sorcar was invited to provide entertainment for the Opening Ceremony of a Colorado Crush and Grand Rapids Rampage football game in 2005. Sorcar treated the crowd of 22,000 with his laser extravaganza using the football field as his screen. The theme was, "Feel Like a Kid Again." A young boy's dream of the football game was simulated in three distinctly separate media—laser, video and live action. Projected from five levels up, the laser show not only captured the spirit of the game, but cheered the players along to an emotional win!

(top) Image of the Pepsi Center in Denver, Colorado, USA.
(bottom) Image of a child dreaming of a football game. The image spanned over 15 yards.

Back to the Future

The Grand Opening Ceremony of the *Gold Rush XVIII* convention of the Gold Wing Touring Association (GWTA) of Indianapolis, Indiana, took place at the Two Rivers Convention Center in Grand Junction, Colorado, USA. Manick Sorcar's laser show, *Back to the Future,* combined with live action on stage, was the highlight of the event. Built on the concept of Steven Spielberg's 1985 hit movie, the eccentric scientist, Old Doc, took off in his Delorean which was magically transformed into a laser-animated Honda Gold Wing motorcycle for an astonishing time travel.

The fun-filled event of the world famous club hosted an estimated 2000 members, and ran for four days, July 18 through 21, 2005.

(top) An image of the bald eagle that travels back in time to reach the era of the 1950's.
(bottom) The Delorean automobile of the movie *Back to the Future* transforms into a Honda Gold Wing, as depicted in this image.

"... It was a great pleasure to meet you, partly because you are your father's (P.C. Sorcar) son, and more because you are you... to see your patriotic laser-animation show, you have successfully brought together art and science in a very original way. I wish you success in your further endeavours and hope to meet you and see your show again in the future."

Dr. R. Chidambaram
Principal Scientific Advisor to the Government of India

Horizon and Beyond

 Kshitij 2006 was the annual mega event of the Indian Institute of Technology in Kharagpur, India. It was a celebration of today's Indian youth. At this glorious event, Manick Sorcar presented a 22-minute laser show titled *Horizon and Beyond*. It was an extravaganza of laser graphics, overhead laser spectacles, with intelligent lighting synchronized with its story and background music. Inside the Tagore Open Air Theater (TOAT), thousands experienced a visual journey from 2500 BC India to 2006, all depicted by 3-D overhead laser spectacle and on-screen graphics. The audience saw how IIT Kharagpur evolved from its humble beginnings to becoming India's leading technological institute. "Absolutely impressive! I am still wondering how you managed the laser to do those fascinating waves overhead," said Professor B. K. Mathur, Head of the Department of Physics & Meteorology, IIT, Kharagpur. After the show, Sorcar was congratulated by Professor Jacky Baltes of the University of Manitoba, Canada; Dr. Farrokh Mistree, Professor in Woodruff School of Mechanical Engineering at the Georgia Institute of Technology; IIT Professor M. Chakraborty, Dean of Alumni Affairs.

(top) Overhead laser on display during Sorcar's presentation at *Kshitij 2006*. The historic moments were captured by many with their digital cameras.

(*top*) Manick Sorcar receiving the Honorary Plaque from Professor Sunando Das Gupta, Co-Chairman, *Kshitij 2006,* IIT, Kharagpur.
(*bottom*) At the guest dinner after the show, Sorcar with his wife, Shikha; Dr. R. Chidambaram; Professor M. Chakraborty of IIT, Kharagpur; and Jacky Baltes of the University of Manitoba, Canada.

A Painting Brush: Made With Laser

In 2006, Jadavpur University had invited Sorcar to be a guest lecturer for their *New Generation Light Sources & Applications* seminar in Kolkata, India. In his speech, *A Painting Brush Made With Laser,* Sorcar explained the fundamentals of laser, and how the narrow, strong beam of light could be tamed and used as a paintbrush in space. He also explained the concept of moving animation with laser, and provided information on a slew of new lighting equipment, such as actuators, galvos, X-Y scanners, and Poly Chromatic Acousto Optic Modulators (PCAOM's). The seminar was followed by a laser demonstration titled, "Reaching the Infinity."

This was the second honor from Jadavpur University for Sorcar; the first being his books used as university texts for illuminating engineering courses.

(top) Sorcar alongside academic members of Jadavpur University at the *New Generation Light Sources & Applications* seminar. (From left to right) Professor Ajay Ghosh, Department of Optics & Photonics at the University of Calcutta; wife Shikha; Mr. Rajat S. Mandal, Senior General Manager of Osaram company; Professor S.K. Sanyal, Pro Vice Chancellor; Professor K. Goswami, Joint Director of SISED; and Dr. S. Mazumdar, Convener.
(bottom) Sorcar with students at the Illumination Laboratory of Jadavpur University, Kolkata, India.

The show was such a success, it was shown a record 78 times in 30 days at the theme park, attracting over 140,000 spectators.

"We had approximately 25,000 visitors today (Dec. 26). Generally, during this time (year-end holidays) we have around 10,000 to 12,000 visitors."

Souma Roychowdhury
Spokesperson for
Nicco Park
Article in *Express India*
India

LaserToons

In late 2005 through early 2006, for the first time, the Indian audience got to watch a laser show designed for the entire family, in a native language of India. The venue was Nicco Park, popularly known as the Disneyland of India—the perfect place to stage Manick Sorcar's *LaserToons*. *LaserToons* was a 30-minute extravaganza of colorful graphics, animation, and three-dimensional laser-magic in space, based on four popular children's songs that were written by Sorcar and sung by his two U.S.-born daughters Piya and Payal, then 8 and 5. It was shown on a massive tri-screen inside a custom-built mega-auditorium. *Ananda Bazar Patrika*, the leading newspaper of Bengal, listed it as one of the few shows that rocked the city. A record 78 shows were shown in one month, each with a packed house.

(top) An image of the logo used for Sorcar's laser show.
(bottom) Crowds eagerly await Sorcar's *LaserToons* at Nicco Park in India.

"Laser-animation is cutting-edge technology that relates to children of the 21st century directly. My goal was to bring that magic in *LaserToons*."

Manick Sorcar

(top) Sorcar explaining his work with laser to the audience, before the shows. Many of them came hours before the show to secure a seat on the ground.
(bottom) The show had attracted a wide variety of audience, from Buddhist monks (left) to Mother Teresa nuns (right).

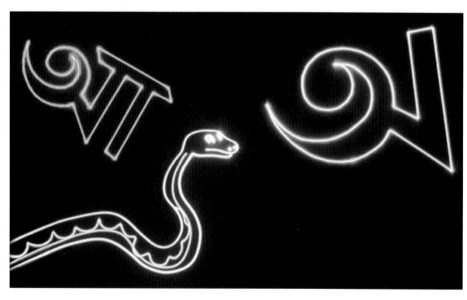

"Laser breathes life into local toons...
the show at Nicco Park will show
many young Tom & Jerry or Harry
Potter fans that there is much in our
own closet worth 'toon'-ing into."

-*The Telegraph*
India
December 21, 2006

"Magic of lasermania: Manick Sorcar conjures up breathtaking shows using
desi toon characters."

-*Asian Age*
India
December 2006

(top left) Mr. Rabbit in *Chuchho Kattaar Biye* (Wedding of the Mole Leader) at Disneyland.
(top right) A laser image used in Sorcar's show.
(bottom left) A python races with the Bengali alphabet in *Oi Ajagar*.
(bottom right) The wedding couple.

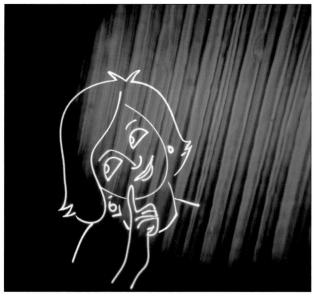

(top) Publicity billboard used by Nicco Park.
(inset & bottom left) Scenes from *The Astronaut*.
(bottom right) Billboards on highway.

Live Action Shows

Having an early exposure to stage shows, Sorcar started to create many live action shows that involved a large troupe including the whole family. While wife, Shikha, supervised the costumes and production coordination, daughters Piya and Payal choreographed fusion dance routines that reflect both Indian and western cultures. His shows were a spectacular mix of elaborate set-ups and lights with live action to which Sorcar added laser effects in his future productions.

(top) Sorcar's daughters, Piya and Payal, the choreographers of Sorcar's world touring shows.
(inset) Sorcar making some crucial adjustments to his intelligent lighting fixtures prior to a show.
(bottom left) One of Sorcar's shows in the early-80's for India Association of Colorado.

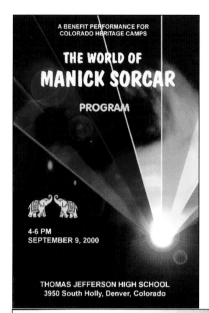

In a letter addressed to the Sorcar family:

"Over the years, I have written many thank you letters to you, and others, in recognition of the valuable contributions given to Colorado Heritage Camps, Inc. However, never in all those years have I been so full of awe and gratitude as I am as I write this letter to you. What you did for CHC, Inc., and in particular, for the East Indian Heritage Camp cannot be matched, and I daresay, will not be surpassed by any other donor.

'The World of Manick Sorcar' was a spectacular production, professional, entertaining and educational. I know the audience enjoyed themselves immensely and it looked as though the performers did as well, especially our very lucky adopted children, who had the chance of a lifetime working with you all..."

Pam Sweetser
Executive Director
Colorado Heritage Camps, Inc.
USA
September 25, 2000

Heritage Camps

The mission of Colorado Heritage Camps, Inc. is "to provide educational, cultural, and family related experiences, which support the healthy development of families formed by adoption with children from diverse heritages. Through shared experiences, each Heritage Camp provides children and families with a sense of community and individual identity." Manick Sorcar and his family were actively involved in the East India Heritage Camps since its inception in the early-90's—where at the annual camps, for almost ten years, Sorcar taught painting, wife Shikha gave cooking classes, and daughters Piya and Payal taught Indian dances to the adopted children. On September 9, 2000, Sorcar presented a special two-hour benefit program for Colorado Heritage Camps, where the adopted children took part under his direction. The show was highly successful and its proceeds were donated to Colorado Heritage Camps.

(top left) Brochure cover of Sorcar's show, a benefit performance for Colorado Heritage Camps.
(top right) Children of East India Heritage Camp watch Sorcar's animation on a monitor.
(bottom left) Proceeds from the special show donated to Colorado Heritage Camp.
(bottom right) Piya and Payal Sorcar teaching traditional and fusion dances to adopted children of India at the East Indian Heritage Camp.

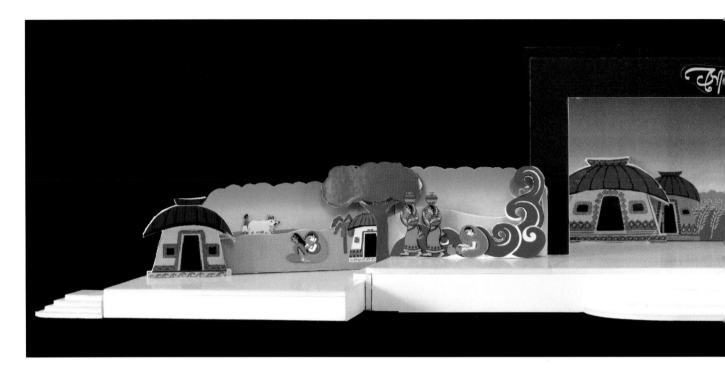

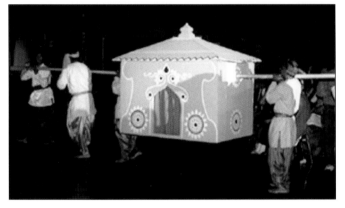

NABC 1999 (Santa Clara)

  Manick Sorcar was invited by the 19th Annual North American Bengali Conference (NABC) committee to help them design a stage with state-of-the-art lighting. He was also requested to conceptualize and direct the Grand Opening Ceremony in a unique fashion.

  Under his direction, 70 graceful performers took part in the Opening Ceremony, including former Miss Universe, Sushmita Sen, on a 120-foot wide performance arena consisting of five stages in multilevel with elaborate three-dimensional stage settings, stylized artwork, intriguing lighting—altogether representing an artistic, yet typical village scene, meeting the NABC theme of "Sonar Bangla" (Golden Bengal).

(top) The model of a 120-foot wide, 5-stage performing arena, designed by Manick Sorcar.
(bottom left) A group of dancers take their turn to perform on different parts of the stage.
(bottom right) Amidst popular songs and to the surprise of the audience, a palanquin is dramatically carried on to the stage all the way from the rear end of the auditorium.

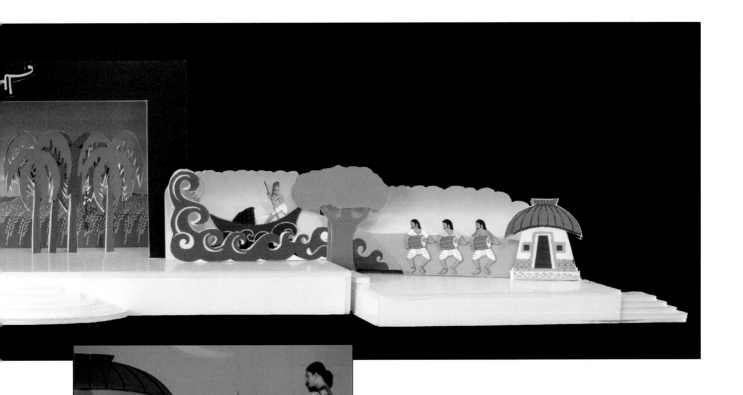

"Denver-based Manick Sorcar's superb stage was a sight to behold. Sorcar had exquisitely hand painted all the rural icons so dear to Bengalis—drummers, a pair of village maidens seated in a typical pose with one doing the hair of the other, a boatman, tall palms, a billowing paddy field, even two huts on two sides. Instead of a standard 40-foot stage, all of this was set in a huge 120-foot, five-level stage that was quite a spectacle."

-India West
USA
July 9, 1999

(middle) Former Miss Universe, Sushmita Sen, acts as the Bengali Lady who lights the lamp.
(bottom) Manick Sorcar takes a bow amidst the appreciation given by Sushmita Sen, other participants and the cheering crowd for the superb direction of the Opening Ceremony.

Flames of Fusion

On October 8, 2000, Manick Sorcar and his troupe performed at the prestigious Denver Center for the Performing Arts as a part of the Colorado Performing Arts Festival. The show titled *Flames of Fusion* was directed by Sorcar and choreographed by his daughter Piya Sorcar—incorporating fusion dances of the East and West and was an expression of today's "Generation X." Carrying a flavor of the preceding, highly successful show, The World of Manick Sorcar, it enchanted the audience with music, dance, drama and magic integrated with spectacular stage settings and state-of-the-art lighting.

Ms. Shirley MacLaine, the legendary Hollywood film star was awarded the Mayor's Lifetime Achievement Award at the Buell Theater next door, at the Performing Arts Center. Invited by The Denver Film Society, Manick Sorcar and his wife, Shikha, were 'special guests' at the occasion. It was a very heartwarming reunion for both Ms. MacLaine and Manick Sorcar as the event flashed back memories of 1964, when she had made a special trip to Calcutta, India to meet Sorcar's father, legendary magician Late P.C. Sorcar, backstage at Calcutta New Empire Theater.

(top left & right) A scene from Sorcar's show at the Denver Center for Performing Arts (DCPA).
(middle right) The Sorcar family with Cleo Parker-Robinson, Executive Director of Dance Ensemble.
(bottom left) Film star, Ms. Shirley MacLaine, felicitates Late P.C. Sorcar backstage in the New Empire Theater, Calcutta, in November, 1964.
(bottom right) Manick and Shikha Sorcar alongside Shirley MacLaine at the Denver Center of the Performing Arts on October 21, 2000.

"Aside from his incredible laser fantasy of 'India Forever,' Manick skillfully and artfully combined magic with traditional Indian dances, colorful props and wonderful cast. One has to see it to truly enjoy his unbelievable production... It was truly amazing and fantastic!"

Philippine/Asian-American Times
USA

Rhythm of 2001

A two-hour extravaganza of dance-drama-magic in combination with laser was the highlight of *Rhythm of 2001*, performed at Teikyo Loretto Heights Theater in Denver, Colorado, USA on September 9, 2001. The mammoth show contained more than 50 participants and the motto of the show was "Kids 4 Kids: Working together to raise awareness about child abuse." It was an Indian-American extravaganza with fusion dances, drama, comedy and magic integrated with sophisticated, colorful laser-animation and state-of-the-art lighting that kept the audience spellbound for the entire two hours. During the Opening Ceremony, in addition to having laser graphics on a floating screen on stage, Sorcar introduced exciting beam and fan effects to shoot overhead, followed by spectacular moving, patterned lights from intelligent lighting systems throughout the show.

(top) *Sorcarland*, a dance piece that blends with magic.
(middle) A lamp dance rooted in village India.
(bottom) A scene from the laser show.

Kids 4 Kids:
Working together to raise awareness about child abuse

Manick Sorcar Productions

PRESENTS

Rhythm of 2001

1 PM and 5 PM
September 9, 2001

Teikyo Loretto Heights Theater
3001 South Federal Blvd. Denver, CO 80236

"He envisioned the stage production that would use that kind of lighting (laser), alongside live action and dancers, all together in one show that would celebrate his heritage... for Sorcar, the son of Indian magician, P.C. Sorcar, from vision to reality was just a matter of time."

The Denver Post
USA
September, 2000

(top left) Manick Sorcar with a young member of the audience in a scene from the show.
(bottom left) Sorcar donates his show proceeds to Eleanor Glover, Representative for the Public Support Division of the American Red Cross. On left is wife Shikha.
(top right) The cover of the program brochure for *Rhythm of 2001*.
(bottom right) The Sorcars donating their show proceeds to Andy Sirotnak and Stephanie Stronks Knapp of the Colorado Professional Society on the Abuse of Children (COPSAC).

Laser Art & Live-Animation

Combining live action with laser-animation, Sorcar developed a new form of artistic expression through a technique called "SorcarScope." This method allowed live performers to interact with laser-animation figures freely. These performances had received rave reviews and introduced Sorcar into a whole new realm of art—one where he was able to combine his love of art and science into one creative canvas. Along with the live-stage performances, Sorcar's cartoon animation were also shown during many of the shows to the thrill of the youngsters in the audience.

Dancing With My Soul

It is the story of a skilled dancer who lost her confidence prior to a show. She sits, sad and confused, and then her soul emerges to encourage her to try again. The soul shows the dancer the forgotten steps, and they dance together until she regains her confidence. The life-size soul was done with laser-animation. *Dancing With My Soul* was a Finalist for the 2004 ILDA Artistic Award in the category for best use of laser with live action on stage.

(top) Piya Sorcar posing with her laser soul.
(bottom) The two dancers mirror each other in rhythmic motion.

Laser - Magic

At the banquet gala of the 2001 Indian American Cultural Association (IACA), Sheraton Hotel in Atlanta, Georgia, USA Sorcar put up a half hour show choreographed by the Sorcar sisters. It was a mix of classical Indian and western dance, lighting and laser with 'SorcarScope' as the highlight.

(top) Sorcar with his two daughters, Piya and Payal, at the beginning of the show.
(inset) An abstract laser scene from the show.
(bottom) Piya Sorcar dancing with her laser soul in perfect union.

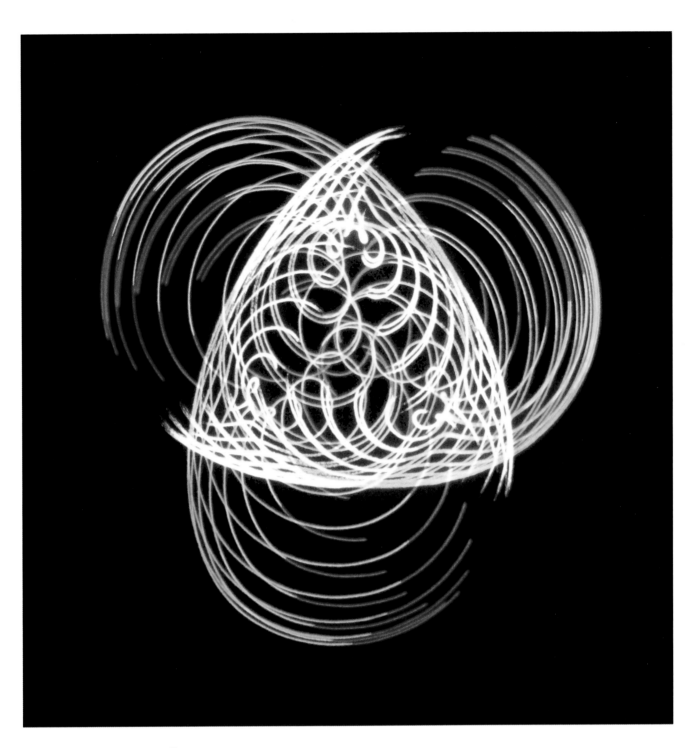

Mesmerizing Lines

An abstract scene captured from the moving animation of laser.

International Congress on Child Abuse & Neglect

Protection of child abuse victims has been a subject close to Sorcar's heart. The four day mega-event held at the Adam's Mark Hotel in Denver, Colorado, USA in 2002 was jointly presented by the International Society for the Prevention of Child Abuse and Neglect (ISPCAN), Kempe Children's Foundation, and Kempe Children's Center. Through his laser show, Sorcar raised funds towards the protection for victims of child abuse.

(top left) A scene from *Dancing With My Soul.* The item was so popular, it was performed in many of Sorcar's shows.
(top right) The Sorcar family with Richard Krugman M.D., Congress Chairman at the International Congress on Child Abuse & Neglect.
(bottom) Sorcar's speech prior to the show.

"Sorcar Honored for Technological Achievement

Sorcar Jr. (Manick Sorcar) honored for integrating magic with technology. Manick Sorcar, son of legendary Indian magician P.C. Sorcar Sr., has been honored by the University of Missouri, Kansas City, for using technology to promote Indian culture."

The Linking Page
The Linking Ring
USA
August 1, 2002

Banga Mela

In 2002, Sorcar directed the Opening Ceremony of *Banga Mela*, the "Festival of Bengal." Held at the Performing Arts Center of the University of Missouri in Kansas City, Missouri, USA the show included a Lamp Dance, followed by *Bengal Forever*—a ten-minute laser show capturing Bengal's 2000 year-old history. Sorcar presented a scene from rural West Bengal on stage with stylized, full-size decorated huts, surrounded by waves, hundreds of lit lamps, a crescent moon and twinkling stars—all designed by him. It concluded with *Celebrate Bengal*, a series of nostalgic songs and dances choreographed by his daughters, and performed by Sorcar's dance troupe. Sorcar also received an honorary plaque from Dr. Martha Gilliland, former Chancellor of the University of Missouri for his distinguished service in promoting Indian culture through his animation and artwork.

(top) Troupes of dancers in colorful outfits fill the stage along with spectacular laser lighting.
(left) Sorcar Dance Troupe with Randy Pembrook, Dean of Conservatory of the University of Missouri, Kansas City, USA.
(right) Performers in a scene from the "Festival of Bengal."

"... A two-hour tantalizing show that uplifts the spirit and helps to bring people together in greater Cincinnati."

Mayor Charlie Luken
Cincinnati, Ohio, USA
September 9, 2002

Harmony 2002

At the Procter & Gamble Hall in Cincinnati, Ohio, USA Sorcar directed *Harmony 2002,* a fund-raiser for the awareness of AIDS. The two-hour event was themed on harmony, reflecting on the September 11 attacks. Also included were *Anarkali,* which portrayed the Mughal era of India, and *Underwater Fantasy,* a story depicting the rescue of a fairy queen in an underwater setting, with the aid of spectacular lighting.

(top) A scene from *Underwater Fantasy.*

"Like da Vinci, Sorcar
is nothing short of a
renaissance man. By
combining magic, laser
beams, animation, computer
graphics, and traditional
Indian dance, Sorcar
manages to create an awe-
inspiring Indian fantasy
world."

Paul Moran
The News Record
Weekend Edition
Cincinnati, Ohio, USA
September 26-29, 2002

(top) Scenes from *Anarkali*.

"Manick Sorcar has established
himself as the monarch of
lighting art."

Ganashakti
December 17, 2002

Sorcarama

The people of Kolkata, India were witness to yet another Sorcar spectacle. Shown in 2003, *Sorcarama* combined his animated film *Rule of Twenty-One* and his works in laser/live action with *Dancing With My Soul* and *Synergy* into one spectacular presentation.

(top left) People at the lounge of Uttam Mancha Theater, awaiting the show.
(top right) Button from the *Sorcarama* show.
(bottom) Scenes from *Sorcarama*.

"...He has created a different type of magic with color, art and laser light... in the New Year, we salute the New magician of the New age."

Protidin
Sunday Section
India
January 5, 2003

"Creating brilliance... A two-hour laser animation and live action extravaganza, choreographed by daughters Piya and Payal, this is a first of its kind show in India."

The Week
India
January 19, 2003

(top left) "The Hypnotizers are Here," said the caption of the large image of the Sorcar family in *Ananda Bazar Patrika*, India, welcoming them to the great city prior to the opening of *Sorcarama*.
(top right) Payal and Piya Sorcar with Neha Pall, the three key dancers of the show.
(middle right) A dance scene from *Synergy*.
(bottom right) A laser art used in the show.

"... Manick made a conscious choice to
move away from his family profession of
magic. Today he glows in his own genius."

Ananda Bazar Patrika
India
April, 2003

"... Thank you for promoting cultural
awareness and for sharing your heritage
with others."

Bill Smith
Mayor of Edmonton, Alberta, Canada
April, 2003

LASER ANIMATION
MANICK SORCAR

Bangla Utsab (Festival of Bengal)

In 2003, *Bangla Utsab* (Festival of Bengal) took place in the ballroom of Sheraton Grand Hotel in Edmonton, Alberta, Canada. His Highness Bill Smith, the Honorable Mayor of Edmonton, graced the occasion with his presence. Manick Sorcar directed the evening's Grand Opening Ceremony. It began with *Bengal Forever: A Laser Fantasy*, capturing 2000 years of Bengal's rich history. This was followed by a series of nostalgic folk songs and dances from Bengal, jazzed up with fantastic laser and lighting effects.

(top) Dancers performing a nostalgic Bengali dance.
(bottom) Swami Vivekananda in a poster from *Bengal Forever: A Laser Fantasy*.

The Grand Opening Ceremony with *Beyond Boundaries* was witnessed by approximately 8,700 people.

Beyond Boundaries (Baltimore)

The 2004 North American Bengali Conference at the Baltimore Convention Center in Baltimore, Maryland, USA picked Manick Sorcar's world traveling troupe to do the Opening Ceremony. Incorporating the talents of 12 Denver dancers and 52 dancers from the Baltimore area, Sorcar's Opening Ceremony was highly anticipated. The hour-long performance took the audience from rural Bengal to the city, and from the city to beyond. The choreographer for the Denver group was Payal Sorcar, and for the Baltimore/Washington, D.C. group it was Jayantee Paine-Ganguly, while Piya Sorcar was the general dance director of the entire show.

(top) The dance troupe of *Beyond Boundaries.*
(bottom left) A scene from a Bengali folk dance.
(bottom right) Dazzling laser fill the Baltimore Convention Center during Sorcar's show.

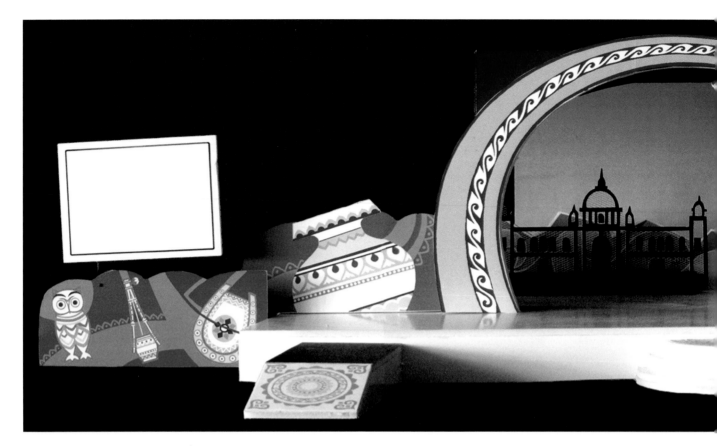

"... His unique presentation of the Opening Ceremony with magnificent choreography, enchanting music, and laser-light-magic thrilled the audience..."

Ananda Bazar Patrika
India
July 4, 2004

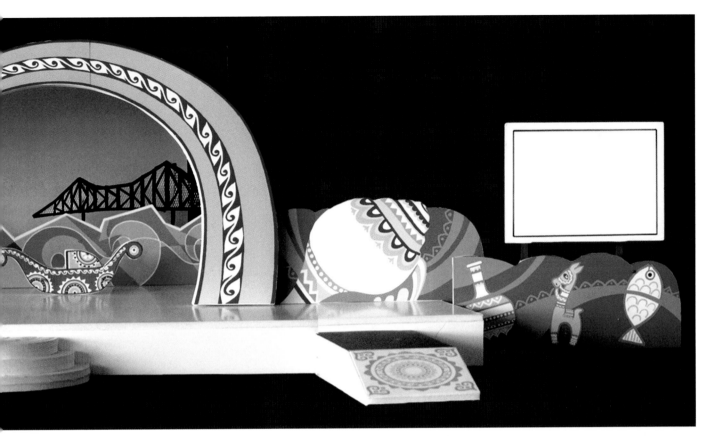

(top) The model of the 80-foot wide, 3-stage performance arena that was designed by Sorcar.
(bottom left) Traditional Bengali dance in front of elegant stage set.
(middle) Under the direction of Sorcar, film star Rituparna Sengupta acts as herself in a scene of Calcutta.
(bottom right) Set of dancers perform with elegance.

"Manick Sorcar's Opening Ceremony brought a feast to the eyes and kept the audience spellbound with the dramatic performance of 62 artists under laser spectacles..."

Asian TV
News Telecast
USA
July 17, 2004

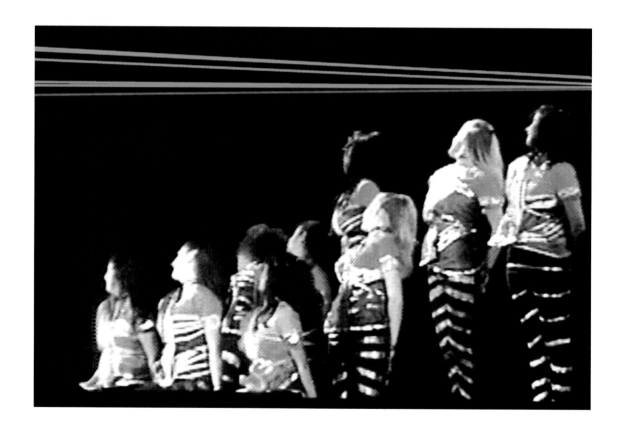

(top) Laser beams shoot out of the Statue of Liberty.
(bottom) A fusion dance synchronized with laser beams above.

Asia Fantasia

   After the tragic events of the Asian Tsunami in 2005, Sorcar participated in *Asia Fantasia*, a fund-raising campaign at the Colorado State University in Fort Collins, Colorado, USA to help raise money towards aid of the affected countries. His team performed *Synergy* and *Underwater Fantasy*, the opening and closing acts of the fund-raiser event.

(top)   A scene from *Underwater Fantasy*.
(bottom)   Group of performers for *Synergy*.

Enlightenment of Buddha

On October 15, 2005, the Silver Jubilee Celebration of the Asian Pacific Development Center took place at the Donald Seawell Ballroom of the Denver Center for Performing Arts in Colorado, USA. Sorcar's *Enlightenment of Buddha* packed with laser-light effects, dance, drama, music and magic, took the audience to 600 B.C. India, and presented the age-old story of Lord Buddha in a completely new form. Here the audience got to experience how the fiercest demon, Mara, was trying to disrupt Buddha's meditation with his power of black magic. All were live actors except for Mara, and his black magic actions that were done by laser. It was a fantastic juxtaposition of the old and the new. The show later received recognition from the International Laser Display Association (ILDA) with the 2005 Artistic Award for best use of laser in live stage performance.

Awards & Accolades

FIRST PLACE *for best use of laser in live stage performance*
2005 ILDA Artistic Award

(top) Evil spirits set the forest into inferno in trying to tempt Siddhartha out of enlightenment in Sorcar's production. The magical fire was created with laser.

(top) Siddhartha is shown meditating under a tree in *Enlightenment of Buddha.*
(bottom left) A section of the audience at the Donald Seawell Ballroom, DCPA.
(bottom right) Denver Mayor John Hickenlooper in praise of the event.

(top) Manick Sorcar receives the ILDA 2005 Artistic Award for his stage show *Enlightenment of Buddha*. He won First Place for best use of laser in live stage performance. From left, Dirk Baur, President of the ILDA, Manick Sorcar, and Patrick Murphy, Executive Director of the ILDA. The award ceremony took place on March 13, 2006 at the Hotel Le Conchiglie in Rimini, Italy.
(bottom) Manick and Shikha in front of Hotel Le Conchiglie, Rimini, Italy.

Optoelectronics Manufacturing PAGE S1

LaserFocusWorld

MAY 2006   WWW.LASERFOCUSWORLD.COM

INTERNATIONAL RESOURCE FOR TECHNOLOGY AND APPLICATIONS IN THE GLOBAL PHOTONICS INDUSTRY

Octave-spanning laser probes physics PAGE 65

▶ Ti:sapphire lasers go modular PAGE 91
▶ New tools support MEMS metrology PAGE 97
▶ Quantum cryptography beefs up security PAGE 109

optoelectronic **world**news   May, 2006

ENTERTAINMENT LASERS

Laser-staged 'Enlightenment of Buddha' wins 2005 ILDA Award

"Enlightenment of Buddha," by Manick Sorcar, an extravaganza of dance, drama, and magic amid various forms of intelligent lighting, life-size laser-animation, and 3-D laser effects in space, captured the *2005 ILDA Artistic Award* (the industry equivalent of Hollywood's Oscars) for "best use of lasers in a live stage performance" in March, at the 2006 annual conference of the International Laser Display Association in Rimini, Italy.

Describing himself as an engineer-animator-laserist, Sorcar is the author of three university texts in lighting, and CEO and president of Sorcar Engineer-

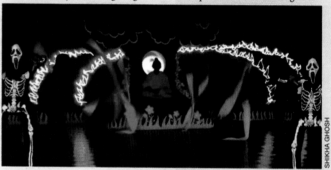

ing (Denver, CO), an electrical-engineering and lighting-design firm, whose projects include the lighting designs for Denver International Airport, Colorado Convention Center, sport centers in Japan, and numerous stage shows. Sorcar is also an accomplished animator.

The "Enlightenment of Buddha" story takes the audience to India in 600 B.C., where a meditating Siddhartha Gautama (whom the world would later know as Buddha) sat under a Banyan tree in Gaya, India, closed his eyes, gathered all of his senses, and began to meditate. Peace was elusive, however, because the fiercest of demons, Devaputra Mara, set out to ruin the young monk's meditation.

All characters in Sorcar's production were live actors except for Mara and his magic, which were created using a variety of lasers, including three 3.5 W argon-krypton lasers for color graphics, two 2.5 W Nd:YAG lasers, and one 100 mW Nd:YAG laser for graphics and effects. All of the lasers were programmed through a set of computers to project in a predetermined, coordinated manner. The magic involved a wide variety of characters and applications, including wild pets (running skeletons of dogs and cats), ghosts, lightning bolts, and rays of enlightenment.

The task was challenging, Sorcar said, because the live performers had to interact precisely with laser graphics. Perhaps the most challenging was the last scene, in which the frustrated ghosts (live performers) with waving flames in hand set the whole forest afire—all of which was created with lasers. In this dramatic scene, the audience saw a peaceful Lord Buddha meditating with his eyes closed, totally undisturbed—amid the surrounding of a burning forest full of flames of ghostly fire (see figure).

"Enlightenment of Buddha" was first performed last October at the Denver Center for Performing Arts, Colorado, for the 25th anniversary of the Asian Pacific Development Center. Attended by many dignitaries from across the country, it was praised by Denver Mayor John Hickenlooper and received rave reviews from the press and media.

Hassaun A. Jones-Bey

(left) Front cover of the May 2006 edition of *LaserFocusWorld* magazine. Sorcar's *Enlightenment of Buddha* was reviewed for its technical aspects, and it was in a featured article in their Optoelectronic World News section. *(right)* Haussaun A. Jones-Bey's article on *Enlightenment of Buddha.*

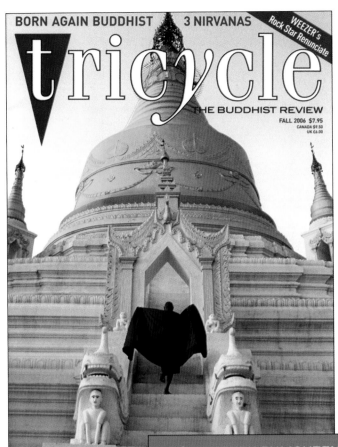

"These focused beams of intense light (laser) have long been standalone wonders of hi-tech entertainment. But Sorcar has earned them the pride of place in an artist's repertoire. For this veteran of thematic laser animations, every production is an ever more breathtaking blend of live action with life-size laser characters."

Harsh Kabra
in "Animate Magic"
The Hindu newspaper
Sunday Magazine
India
June 4, 2006

BUDDHA BUZZ

21ST-CENTURY ENLIGHTENMENT

Let's face it: nothing gets a message across like lasers. Thanks to Manick Sorcar's multimedia show "Enlightenment of Buddha," special effects once confined to rock concerts and all-night raves are now serving the dharma. Winner of the Artistic Award for "best use of laser in a live stage performance" at the 2006 International Laser Display Association Conference in Rimini, Italy, the show integrates live performance, three-dimensional laser effects, and life-size animation. Siddhartha Gautama is shown on his way to enlightenment, despite interference by Mara, who is depicted solely by lasers. "Observing the lack of knowledge of the Americans about India and her culture forced me to . . . do something within my means to present it to the world," Sorcar told the Indian national daily *The Hindu*. Just don't let Mara hit you directly in the eye.

Tricycle
The Buddhist Review, New York, USA
Fall 2006

(*top & inset*) Cover and article on the *Enlightenment of Buddha* of *Tricycle*, The Buddhist Review, New York, USA.

"Through his animation based on *The Panchatan-tra*, Manick Sorcar has put Indian culture in the world map. Today the world knows him even more because of his laser miracles."

Rohit Kulkarni
Aaj Tak
Voice of America

"The genius guy has found a way to combine animation, laser and real people into a performance which is seamless and magical."

Carol Dickinson
Former Executive Director/ Curator
Foothills Art Center
VOA Interview

Voice of America

Manick Sorcar was selected as "one of the highly successful people of Indian origin in America," by Voice of America, Hindi TV, that was featured in their popular program *Duniya* (The World). *Duniya* is telecast nationwide by India's leading TV news channel *Aaj Tak*, which draws an audience of over 30 million households. The exclusive profile on Manick Sorcar was nationally telecast in India on October 1, 2006.

(left) Sorcar interviewed by Rohit Kulkarni, Voice of America.
(top right) Rohit Kulkarni, TV Reporter/Producer, speaks about Sorcar during telecast.
(bottom right) Carol Dickinson in an interview with Voice of America, on Manick Sorcar.

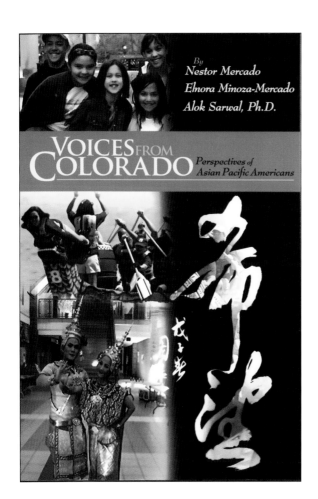

Art in Multi-Media

Manick Sorcar

In 1997, "The Denver Post" addressed him as *"The Animation Man."* In 1998, Colorado's "Jefferson the Magazine" selected him as one of the *"Top 100 People"*, in 2000 he was given the *"Excellence in Arts"* award from the National Federation of Indian American Associations, and in 2005, The *Voice of America* lauded him by telecasting a special feature on him. Welcome to the world of Manick Sorcar, who has been blessed and profusely showered with many talents in art and science, which have given him international recognition and made him the renaissance man of our time. His creative work ranges from being an accomplished electrical engineer, a lighting designer, an author of university texts to _____ ng artist in a variety of _____ fine arts, _____ and _____

"Welcome to the world of Manick Sorcar, who has been blessed and profusely showered with many talents in art and science, which have given him international recognition and made him the renaissance man of our time."

Voices From Colorado
Perspectives of Asian Pacific Americans
p. 236-37
2008

Voices From Colorado & India

(top left) Cover of the book *Voices From Colorado: Perspectives of Asian Pacific Americans*, by Nestor Mercado, Elnora Minoza-Mercado, and Alok Sarwal, Ph.D. (Publisher MIBS, USA) which ran a two-page story on Sorcar.
(top right) The front page of the "Art in Multi-Media" section, listing Manick Sorcar as the first entry.
(bottom) Sorcar with Dr. Debesh Das, the Honorable Minister of Information Technology (IT), West Bengal, India, discussing a proposal of Sorcar on a laser center in Kolkata, India. The meeting took place in Phoenix Arizona, on May 19, 2008 during the Minister's visit to the USA.

FINAL ACT: *Family Moments—then...*